Gender Construction in Kays Catalogues: 1920 to the New Millennium

Edited by
Barbara M. Mitra and Rachel E. Johnson

Cambridge Academic

First edition published by Cambridge Academic, The Studio, High Green, Gt. Shelford, Cambridge CB22 5EG.

ISBN 1-903-499-82-8
978-1-903499-82-5

Printed and bound in the United Kingdom by
4Edge Ltd, 7a Eldon Way Industrial Estate, Hockley, Essex, SS5 4AD.

Contents

Preface

In May 2012, staff from the Information and Learning Services Department successfully applied for JISC funding to run a short project promoting the Kays Archive held in the Research Collections at the University of Worcester, UK.

Six months later, thanks to our outstanding Project Manager Jenni Waugh and her two able assistants, who worked magic in such a short space of time, the World of Kays website, containing 1500 images and memories of Kays from the community, was up and running.

After a number of events, the Project was brought to a conclusion with a successful academic conference which generated interest across the country and drew a wide cross section of people both from academic and non-academic communities. The papers presented at this conference, together with additional contributions, have become this book.

This book therefore covers a wide spectrum of disciplines, ranging from social history, through media and advertising to children's literature, all focused on the theme of gender. Such a resource could equally focus on any number of themes which demonstrates the richness, depth and quality of material available. With those exciting possibilities in mind, we look forward to the future use of this unique resource.

The World of Kays website can be accessed at http://www.worldofkays.org/ where the images can be viewed alongside the following chapters. The search function allows users to find material on specific topics and particular years whilst the stories and blogs provide some interesting insights into how Kays Catalogue was used and highlight nostalgia for the Catalogue.

A visit to the Kays Archive can be arranged by contacting researchcollections@worc.ac.uk. Researchers or anyone interested in investigating the wealth of material, both print and objects, held within the archive are always welcome.

Rachel Johnson
Worcester, June 2014.

Acknowledgments

There are a number of people we would like to thank for their part in the production of this book.

Firstly, thanks to our contributors, whose patience whilst the work was in incubation and whose quick response to our queries was exemplary. Special thanks go to Sam Hammond, experienced indexer based at Duke University, for his generous offer to provide an index for the book. Thanks to Nicoleta Cinpoes for giving up valuable time to act as Barbara's 'critical friend'. We must also acknowledge the part played by Mr Bernard Mills in providing the material for research when he deposited the Kays Archive at the University of Worcester in order to make it available for research. Also, thanks to Jenni Waugh, Project Manager for the JISC funded World of Kays Project, without whom the website and conference would not have materialised.

Finally, Barbara and Rachel would like to thank each other for being such mutually congenial co-workers, and from Rachel, Barbara's lead on this project has made Rachel's contribution a pleasure.

Contributors

Professor Maggie Andrews is Professor of Cultural History at the University of Worcester who has taught in adult, higher and further education for over twenty-five years. Her research covers the social and cultural history of twentieth century Britain with a particular focus on popular culture, domesticity and femininity. She is the author of a feminist history of the Women's Institute movement, *The Acceptable Face of Feminism* (Lawrence and Wichart 1998), and more recently *Domesticating the Airwaves: Broadcasting, Domesticity and Femininity* (Continuum 2012). Her publications also include co-edited with Mary Talbot: a collection of essays exploring women's relationship with consumer culture in the twentieth century *All the World and Her Husband* (Continuum 2000) and with Sallie McNamara *Women and Media 1900 to the Present: Feminism and Femininity* (Routledge 2014).

Dr Kate Flynn recently completed her PhD at the University of Worcester, where her thesis focused on Constructions of the Fat Child in British Juvenile Fiction, 1960-2010. Her research interests include children's literature, comics for girls, and accessible formats for blind and partially sighted children. She works as a research officer for a charity.

Dr Rachel E. Johnson is Associate Researcher with the International Forum for Research into Children's Literature at the University of Worcester, UK. She was formerly the Research Librarian responsible for the management of the Kays Archive.

Dr Mehreen Mirza is a senior lecturer in the Institute of Humanities and Creative Arts at the University of Worcester, and teaches on the BA Sociology programme. Her main research (and teaching) interests are in the fields of gender, 'race'/ethnicity and education. She co-edited a collection on *Teaching Gender and Sexualities in the Twenty-first Century* published by the Higher Education Academy's Subject Centre for Sociology, Anthropology & Politics in 2011. Mehreen is the co-editor of the *Worcester Journal of Learning and Teaching.*

Dr Barbara Mitra is a Senior Lecturer in Media and Cultural Studies at the University of Worcester. Her research interests focus on gender issues and she has published in the areas of children, newsreaders and new media in relation to gender. She is also interested in teaching issues and has published on using videos in teaching and is the co-editor of the *University of Worcester Learning and Teaching Journal.*

Dr Rachel Ritchie gained her PhD from the University of Manchester in 2011. Her research focuses on personal appearance (fashion, home-dressmaking, beauty) and the home (domestic consumption, interior design and decor) in women's magazines and women's organizations. She is the author of 'Young Women in Woman: Representations of youthful femininity in the "world's greatest weekly for women", 1954-1969' in *Women and the Media: Feminism and Femininity in Britain, 1900 to the Present*, edited by Maggie Andrews and Sallie McNamara (Routledge, 2014) and '"Beauty isn't all a matter of looking glamorous": Attitudes to glamour and beauty in 1950s women's magazines' (*Women's History Review* 2014).

List of Illustrations

// Introduction //

Barbara M. Mitra

This book examines the discourses disseminated through Catalogues, particularly the Kays Catalogue, which was very successful throughout the 20th century in selling fashion and household items to millions of people in Britain. The Kays archive, held by the University of Worcester, and available to researchers onsite, also benefits from an online presence. The World of Kays Website consists of 1500 digitised images from the Catalogue spanning over eighty years, from as early as 1913 and continuing up to the last days of the printed Catalogue in 2000. The images provide an invaluable resource for academics and researchers interested in the ideologies and discourses promoted through advertising for fashion, toys and other household items. Mayne (2000: 408) notes that 'advertising both reflects and influences cultural values and impacts people's views of themselves as well as others' and Kays Catalogue provides an historical record of the discourses of advertising in relation to gender, reflecting cultural values and impacting on people's perception of themselves and others in relation to gender. One of the main themes that runs throughout this book is the gendered nature of advertising in the Catalogue, which reinforces a binary perception of gender as male and female being different and relational to each other.

Kays Catalogue

Kays began its life in 1890 as Kays of Worcester, a strict cash with order business, selling products to customers who subscribed to Kays. Worcester has historically been associated with Kays, and its famous landmark, Worcester Cathedral, has featured on the front cover of a number of its issues. Kays Catalogue became hugely popular when it began selling mainstream fashion in the 1920s and this sustained the Catalogue for much of the twentieth century. Towards the end of that era, the Catalogue began to suffer a decline and was taken over by GUS (Great Universal Stores) in 2000. GUS sold the mail order company in 2003 and in 2004 Kays merged with Littlewoods and became known as K&Co (see the Kays Heritage Group website).

Kays Catalogue and Advertising

Essentially, the Catalogue advertised clothing, toys and various household items for people to buy on hire purchase terms, that is, buy now and pay later. This

(Kays Catalogue, 1927: 360, Autumn and Winter)

method made items that were unaffordable available to many people – despite the high interest rates. This book focuses on the discourses that were promoted through the images and words that accompany the various items on sale. Whilst accepting that advertising is everywhere, it is perhaps because of this ubiquity that we may pay less attention to the influence that advertising has upon us. The discourses at work in advertising may subtly influence how people think about themselves and may also influence behaviour. There is a wealth of literature written about gendered discourses in advertising and audience responses to these; this volume, on the other hand, does not make its main concern how audiences respond to the discourses that are presented through the Catalogue. Rather it is concerned with analysing the actual discourses promoted through Kays Catalogue. Although one of the chapters highlights resistance to messages in Catalogues, this point is made through fictional writing rather than through audience research. For the most part, this book focuses on how women, men and children are being addressed in terms of gender through Kays Catalogue.

Women in advertising

Much has been written with regards to gender representation in advertising.

Most academic work published on the topic would address gender stereotypes in advertising at some level. Even readers unfamiliar with such literature will still be aware of advertising images that objectify women and highlight such issues as body image and the size zero debates. There have been feminist challenges to the gendered stereotypes found in many advertisements and media messages. Whilst it is no longer acceptable for women to be shown only as housewives and mothers, there is still much marketing that promotes an idealised image of femininity or a hypersexualised representation of the female body (Dines and Humez, 2011). Thus, whilst there have been distinct changes in social relations over the time period under consideration, these have not always been reflected in advertising. Gender stereotypes are still the mainstay of much advertising (Milestone and Meyer 2012: 67). They include representations that revolve around distinct stages such as finding a man, getting married, having children and domesticity (Negra, 2009). Whilst such images are still present, there have also been shifts in these representations. Women's life stages have become intertwined with how one looks as 'Instead of caring or nurturing or motherhood, it is now possession of a 'sexy body' that is presented as women's key source of identity' (Gill, 2011: 257). This suggests that one may never pass through the life stages unless one possesses the appropriate body. So although there might be a freer femininity in some respects (equal rights and opportunities), there is also a return to more conventional and traditional femininity (Negra, 2009). Kays Catalogue provides a menu from which girls and women may choose their femininity. The range of the Catalogue (albeit a very narrow one) constructs femininity in terms of a thin body image running through all those versions. The Catalogue also clearly represents masculinity and femininity as relational. The myth that *Men are from Mars, Women are from Venus* is reinforced throughout the Catalogue. In addition, the pages for men and women dictate how men and women should look, dress and behave in relation to their gender.

Men and advertising

There are several versions of masculinity or rather masculinities on offer in advertising, from the new man, the new lad, to traditional masculinity (MacKinnon, 2003). In advertising, during the 1990s, men became more used to being represented as sex objects. However, Milestone and Meyer (2012: 144) note that men are not objectified to the same extent as women. Men are still required to 'look good and adhere to standards of style and bodily appearance' (Milestone and Meyer 2012: 144). Nevertheless, there has been a backlash against the softer versions of masculinity and a resurgence of more traditional versions highlighting such characteristics as competitiveness and aggression. Advertising also reinforces differences between men and women highlighting them as relational and different from each other. Again these versions of masculinity can be seen in the Catalogue including the focus on traditional masculinity (such as muscles) as well as softer versions of masculinity (such as the new man and associated ideas). So the Catalogue also reinforces myths about masculinity (MacKinnon, 2003: 89).

Clothing and Identity

Much analysis in this book centres on the clothing and associated images and words in Kays Catalogue. As Hourigan and Bougoure (2012) note, fashion and clothing itself are associated with being (or becoming) feminine and masculine. Fashion is a signifier (Crane, 2012) that is used to convey messages about what it is to be feminine and masculine and is a part of personal and social identity. Whilst Bauman (1996 cited in Crane 2012: 2) argues that in a postmodern society, people avoid constructing specific identities through clothing, fashion advertisements can actually influence the ways in which men and women perceive their femininity and masculinity. By offering specific ranges or versions of masculinities and femininities, Kays Catalogue acts as a regulatory power (Barker 2008: 93) in Foucauldian terms whereby people subject themselves to gender appropriate dressing. The discourses in the Catalogue encourage men and women to put on a performance for an audience, whether that audience is physically present or imagined (Goffman 1990: 32). Thus, the advertisements for clothing provide an insightful source for analysing discourses of gender.

Structure of this book

The chapters in this book focus on different aspects of Kays Catalogue and mail order consumption with a view to how they relate to aspects of gender identity and its different discourses. The first chapter focuses on the words used in advertising toys and clothing commercials for children in the Kays Catalogue. For every decade of the digital Catalogue analysed, clear themes that emerge are discussed; for example, young girls are addressed as mothers to be, from the earliest to the very latest print edition. The discourses suggest that among appropriate roles for young girls, one is becoming 'just like mother.' Another theme present in the Catalogue which is also relatively stable throughout the 80 years was that of being a housewife and doing housework. Despite expectations that this would have changed by the year 2000, such stereotypes remained still very evident. The theme of getting married is also reinforced through other media as well as through the Catalogue. There is also a focus on looks in the Catalogue with make-up being advertised for children, alongside dolls. Boys were clearly not addressed in the same way as girls. In many toy advertisements boys are often shown playing with guns and fighting. In fact, the Catalogue provides a constant and stable discourse about boys in relation to fighting and aggression. Boys are also addressed as having fun, adventure and being active. Toys highlighting occupations for boys include carpentry, engineering and similar occupations. For girls, occupations were suggested through dressing up clothes, including nursing outfits as opposed to superhero ones for boys. There are some clothes and toys that were marketed at both boys and girls, but often these are aimed at younger children. The advertising reveals the hegemonic nature of masculinity even in the advertising aimed at children and reinforces the relational way in which boys and girls are addressed. The chapter highlights how these discourses appear to have persisted throughout the life of the print Catalogue.

The second chapter focuses on the wording surrounding the advertisements for clothing in Kays Catalogue. It highlights how clothing advertising often tends to reproduce discourses associated with gender stereotypes. The chapter draws on analysis of advertisements for every decade that the Catalogue is available in digital format. Throughout the 80 years women are offered a very narrow version of femininity – focused on being pretty, attractive and beautiful mainly through purchasing the clothing advertised. It is something that female customers have to strive to achieve and are made to feel inadequate if they are unable to achieve such an idealised femininity. Whilst men are encouraged to view themselves independently, women are also taught to see themselves from the viewpoint of others. Men tend to be addressed as being active whereas women are addressed as being passive. The advertisements have much to say about conforming to a thin body image (from about 1940s onwards) and if women can't conform they are offered clothing to cover up their non-conformity. Specific occupations are promoted through the Catalogue. For women, these include being a mother, a housewife, and by the later editions it also includes businesswomen, (although they are still more concerned with how they look rather than what they do). The clothing advertisements aimed at men include a wider range of occupations from manual labour, to suits for the office man and leisure wear for the sports man. The issue of weight is treated differently for men, with greater approval and acceptance of a wider variety of male body images. Overall, this chapter highlights that the gendered discourses remain relatively unchanged for men and women over 80 years of the Catalogue.

Chapter 3 focuses on the 1950s and early 1960s of Kays Catalogues, and explores the relationship between purchasing domestic products alongside buying identities, fantasies and aspirations for housewives – such as being a skilled cook or domestic guru. The chapter highlights the domestic as a lived experience as well as a site of imagination. Catalogues like Kays, it is argued, play a role in bridging the gap between the reality in which people live and their idealised lives. This idealised domesticity was a reaction to the austerity during and just after the Second World War. At the same time, the Catalogue provides an alternative to queuing and rationing, giving opportunities for people to purchase items in a more relaxed manner on hire purchase. This chapter provides a snapshot of that particular time period and acknowledges the interweaving of identity and contextual environment as presented in the Kays Catalogue.

In chapter 4, the focus is on the importance of place, namely Worcester City, in relation to Kays Catalogue by case studying twenty covers of Kays Catalogue between 1960 and 1969. Modernity is a key concept throughout this chapter in relation to national identity, as well as overlapping and layering of identities as represented in the Catalogue. The wider context is recognised in relation to magazines although socio-cultural changes do not follow a straightforward linear narrative and minority counter-cultures may be misrepresented as mainstream culture. Worcester differentiated Kays from other Catalogues by emphasising this city with its history, memory and ideology. The discourses and images of Worcester are different from those customarily associated with the Swinging Sixties which focused on London. Whilst Swinging London is represented in the menswear pages in Kays Catalogue, the clothing for women only gives superficial acknowledgement to this urban environment partly because the city is seen as masculine, and not as a safe place for women. There are aspirations attached to the images displayed on the front covers of the Catalogue. Finally, this chapter fore-fronts ideologies of the city, Britishness and identity.

The fifth chapter takes a different stance by placing the role of mail order Catalogues, such as Kays, into the context of novels for teenage girls. The two novels that are explored in this context are *French Letters* and *Waiting for the Sky to Fall*, both written in the 1980s. The chapter explores commodified girlhood as a feminine ideal that girls are encouraged to fulfil through consumerism or rather through the impossible dream of consumerism. In one novel the heroine conforms to the feminine ideal in the mail order Catalogue, whilst in the other novel the consumer imagery is repurposed for imaginative play and the stereotypes are challenged. The Catalogues are seen as a relief from the high street shopping where one is looked at and judged particularly by other females. Clothing in both novels is a source of identity, which either challenges or conforms to gender stereotypes. Class is also important in these novels in relation to identity, clothing and also Catalogue shopping. This chapter offers insightful analysis of the role Catalogue shopping played for young girls in their search for gendered identity.

The final chapter looks to the future and briefly refers to the online version of the *Littlewoods* Catalogue. The chapter notes that women's fashion still focuses on how women look and shows that women are still encouraged to conform to a particular body image. Men's fashion in the online Catalogue still assumes that men will be in paid work. The online Catalogue also highlights the continuation of stereotypes of gender with regards to clothing and toys advertised for children. Boys clothing focuses on what boys will be doing rather than on how they look, whereas girls are still encouraged to be aware primarily of how they look. Thus the active/passive gendered dichotomy is still present in the twenty-first century. There were a few challenges to these stereotypes, with some toys for boys advertised as being for both girls and boys. Dolls, however, were still clearly marketed as being only for girls. This chapter also notes how the internet can challenge the gender stereotypes and refers to campaigns harnessed through new media such as the *Pink Stinks* campaign and the promotion of gender neutral toys in some countries. Finally, this chapter with its focus on the internet provides a new dimension in relation to Catalogue shopping and whilst many of the gendered discourses continue, it argues that there are challenges emerging via new media.

These chapters can be read as standalone studies, focusing on particular themes, or together as one comprehensive analysis of mail order Catalogues, particularly focusing on historical analysis of Kays Catalogue. The theme that draws the various chapters together is the fact that gendered discourses are so prevalent in a Catalogue like Kays, which is teaching customers not only to consume, but to behave according to perceived appropriate gender behaviour. This book adds to the body of knowledge investigating ideologies in mail order Catalogues and consumption, as well as analysing discourses of gender over a long period of time.

References

Barker, C. (2008) *Cultural Studies.* London, Sage.

Crane, D. (2012) Introduction In A. M. Gonzalez and L. Bovone (eds.) *Identities through Fashion. A multidisciplinary Approach.* London, Berg, pp.1-8.

Dines, G. and Humez, J.M. (2011) *Gender, Race, and Class in Media. A Critical Reader.* 3rd edition. London, Sage.

Gill, R. (2007) *Gender and the Media.* Cambridge, Polity.

Goffman, E. (1990) *The Presentation of Self in Everyday Life.* Reprint, London, Penguin.

Gray, J. (2012) *Men are from Mars, Women are from Venus.* Reprint, Harper Element, London.

Hourigan, S. R. and Bougoure, U. (2012) Towards a better understanding of fashion clothing involvement. In *Australasian Marketing Journal*. 20, 127-135.

MacKinnon, K. (2003) *Representing Men: Maleness and Masculinity in the Media.* London, Arnold.

Mayne, I. (2000) The Inescapable Images. Gender and Advertising. *Equal Opportunities International.* Vol. 19(2/3/4), pp.56-61.

Milestone, K. and Meyer, A. (2012) *Gender & Popular Culture.* Cambridge, Polity.

Negra, D. (2009) *What a girl wants. Fantasising the reclamation of self in postfeminism.* London, Routledge.

Websites

World of Kays http://www.worldofkays.org/

Kays Heritage website http://www.kaysheritage.org.uk/

// Chapter 1 //
The Construction of Childhood Gender Identity through Advertising in Kays Catalogue (1920-2000)

Barbara M. Mitra and Mehreen Mirza

Aims

This is the first of two chapters that explore the advertising in Kays Catalogue. This chapter focuses on discourses around toys and clothing for children, whilst the next chapter concentrates on discourses around clothing advertisements for men and women. Mayne (2000: 56) suggests that we are so used to advertising that 'we hardly consider what we see. It is part of our world we are being "sold at" by the advertisers all day and every day.' Thus, we take advertising for granted and are less likely to question some of the more subtle discourses found in advertising. It is also suggested that advertising is part of our socialisation which includes gender socialisation (Mayne, 2000). For children, the discourses found in advertising can be very influential and can inform their notions of gender appropriate behaviour. This chapter considers the potential influence that Kays Catalogue has had on the construction of both female and male childhood identity, and demonstrates the complex intertwining of gender, childhood and consumer culture.

Introduction

The Catalogue has been in print for just over 80 years and this provided an opportunity for us to explore the discourses of gender surrounding commercials aimed at children over this time period. We aimed to investigate whether there were multiple discourses or one dominant discourse in relation to gender and childhood. We also wanted to explore whether these discourses reinforced binary notions of gender. Our research focused on advertising for toys and clothing aimed at children in the Catalogue. This analysis was not concerned with how children responded to the commercials, but rather in analysing how possible gendered discourses are presented through the Catalogue.

Children as a market

The rise of childhood as both a particularly marked stage in the life-cycle (cf. Aries, 1962; Cook, 2004; James et al, 1998) and a consumer group during the late-nineteenth and twentieth centuries (Cook, 2004; 2012) is of great significance and is addressed more fully later on in the chapter. Suffice to say here that the change from viewing the child as having the status of an 'unfinished' person in need of socialization to viewing children as 'finished' people and thus 'legitimate, individualized, self-contained consumers' (Cook, 2004: 3; cf. Russell and Tyler, 2002), means that children of primary school age are a key market for advertisers (Buckingham and Scanlon, 2001). The Kays Catalogue has marketed a wide variety of toys and clothing for children – often with awareness of 'pester power' (Cook, 2004: 146; Lawlor, 2011: 563) where children may ask for products and may influence family consumption.

Advertising and gender representation of children

Advertising has been criticised for its representation of gender (see Verna, 1975; Manstead and McCulloch, 1981; Fowles, 1996) which tends to be rather stereotyped and polarised towards a pink and blue market (Buckingham, 2007).[1] Welch et al. (1979) note that it is the more subtle aspects of commercials which are more likely to be accepted in relation to gender ideology. As Johnson and Young (2002) suggest, customers may be buying toys but they are also simultaneously buying gender ideology along with the toys.

We accept that there can be resistance to discourses: we are not suggesting in any way that children or their parents are 'cultural dopes' (Garfinkel, 1967: 68). As Seiter (1993: 9-10 cited in Cook, 2004: 5) notes, 'We know that children make meanings out of toys that are unanticipated by – perhaps indecipherable to – their adult designers ... Children are creative in their appropriation of consumer goods and media'. However, the prevalence of the discourses around gender, not just amongst the advertisements aimed at children but also adults (see Chapter 2) would suggest that they cannot be ignored in terms of their purpose or effect.

Thematic analysis

Using the digital archive of Kays Catalogue (see http://www.worldofkays.org/) we entered the search terms 'toys' and 'children' for every year that was digitally available. This led to 13 years with 44 successful outcomes for toys which spanned from 1920 to 2000. The authors also wanted to explore the discourses surrounding clothing marketed to girls and boys and therefore the search

1. The arbitrary nature of colour-coding is illustrated by Paoletti and Kregloh (1989: 22-29 cited in Cook, 2004: 101) who argued that the 'girl-pink, boy-blue coding for infants became solidified only after the Second World War in the US'. They also pointed out that 'the Infants Department recommended pink as the colour most suitable for boys in 1918' (Cook, 2004: 101, original emphasis; cf. Entwistle, 2000: 140). There is clearly nothing inherently feminine or masculine about any given colour.

term 'children' was also entered into the digital archive for every decade. Any advertising for clothing was included which led to 110 successful outcomes. The pilot revealed that there was more advertising for clothing available online and so every ten years were included in the study.

Transcription and analysis

The words surrounding these advertisements (both for toys and clothing) were transcribed and recorded for later analysis. After this, the data was analysed using thematic analysis. This 'involves the searching across a data set...to find repeated patterns of meaning' (Braun and Clarke, 2006: 86). The main questions that guided this part of the analysis included whether there were stable discourses consistently repeated over time, or whether the gender discourses changed over time. During this stage, the transcribed data was read and re-read several times as suggested by Fielden, Sillence and Little (2011: 5). Themes were also identified within the transcriptions in relation to girls and boys. The themes that emerged from the data were identified, analysed and defined in more detail (see Ross and Green, (2011: 114) for a similar way of conducting thematic analysis).

Discourses

The following section highlights the themes that were prominent for boys and girls which emerged from the thematic analysis. The discussion begins by highlighting the discourses present in the advertising aimed at girls and then moves on to the analysis of discourses present in the advertising aimed at boys. Towards the end of this chapter the analysis explores toys and clothing that were advertised to both boys and girls.

Discourses of gender: Girls

Girls: Ideal mother

There were clearly themes that emerged which reinforced a binary perception of gender. For example, in relation to girls, one of the dominant discourses that remained relatively static was that of being or becoming a mother. The ideal mother is altruistic and marked by an endless devotion to her family without considering her own needs (Milestone and Meyer, 2012). Being a mother is promoted through looking after dolls which are clearly marketed to girls. From the early editions of the Catalogue to its final year, the advertisements continued to promote motherhood as something natural, to be expected and something that girls should aspire to. For example, the advertisement for a doll in 1939 (p.132) noted 'Mamma's baby Doll...Baby Doll says 'Mamma' and also has natural eyelashes.' So calling the child 'Mamma' reinforces her role as a future mother. The notion of being a mother is also reinforced through advertisements suggesting that the dolls are life-like. In the 1960s Catalogue another advertisement noted 'Beautiful dolls. Life-like to the minutest details' (1960: 702). This enables the child to imagine herself in the position of their mother. Similarly the prams that were advertised alongside the dolls highlight how an ideal mother should behave. A 'Tracy Pram- merrily it rolls along at playtime and folds down at dolly's bedtime' (1973: 1006). This reinforces the role of a mother to put her children to bed, and to look after and nurture their children. The advertisements, therefore, also suggest that such nurturing is appropriate behaviour for a girl. For example, (1980: 923) 'Every little girl will love this delightful cot – ideal for that favourite doll' which suggests to girls that they should love cots and have a favourite doll. Even in 2000, the theme of being a mother came across in the advertisements: 'Girl Doll and Feeding Set. This sweet and loveable baby comes complete with its own elegant little outfit, feeding bottle, soother and nappy, to make playing at mum being great fun' (2000: 1165). The dolls are also life-like to enable girls to know what is involved in being a mother: 'My Pretty Baby Girl. With your help this beautiful baby drinks, wets and cries real tears. Comes complete with bottle and potty' (2000: 1165). This ensures that girls are aware that caring for a baby is part of their role. There is no equivalent doll aimed at boys.

The theme of becoming a mother was also reinforced through the clothing and accessories marketed in the Catalogue. In 1947 for example, there was a 'Kiddies shoulder bag. Here is a shoulder bag just like mummy's' (1947: 86). Similarly in 1953 'We proudly present a handbag that will be of unparalleled appeal to all children aged 4 to 9 years. It is a perfect smaller reproduction of Mother's in real unlined leather' (1953: 156). This notion of being just like mother suggests that this is something girls should aim for. This theme continues with an ideal mother being one that also does the shopping: 'Supermarket trolley and doll. Go shopping just like mummy – room for dolly too' (1980: 922). Another aspect of being a mother is being able to sew. The use of the girl's name in the following advertisement ensures that girls are aware that this is part of their mothering role: 'The Little Betty Kiddies miniature sewing machine' (1967: 1020). These commercials teach young girls that they should want the role of a mother, and that becoming a mother is a gender appropriate role for girls. It also suggests that this is an acceptable future occupation and provides the scripts for girls to enact their gender role. Butler (1990) argues that discourses present themselves through the use of scripts where performativity is not who you are (girl) but something you do (for example, looking after dolls, going shopping or sewing). This is reinforced through the endless repetition of playing with a doll and the surrounding toys (and behaviour) that are perceived as the norm for girls.

Girls: Housework

One theme that was present in the Catalogue and was relatively stable throughout the 80 years was that of being a housewife or women doing housework. At the start of the Catalogue one would expect this theme to be prominent, as highlighted by an advertisement in 1939 that noted: 'Child's sweeper set. The proud little housewife will simply love this realistic sweeper set. Comprising brush with long handle, mop and Mickey Mouse carpet sweeper complete' (1939: 312). In 1967 another advertisement noted: 'Carpet sweeper – a perfect miniature with push button dustpans exactly like the real thing' and also a 'vacuum cleaner for the junior housewife' (1967: 1020). This theme of being a housewife and helping mother do housework continued in 1977: 'Ironing set. Help mummy with the housework with this super set of household tools. Set comprises iron and ironing board, carpet sweeper. Clothes airier and stool' (1977: 934-5). The use of girl models also ensures that girls are aware of whom the commercials are targeting (see Pike and Jennings, 2001). Thus, girls learn that part of being female is doing housework and having pride in how a home looks. Despite assumptions that such commercials might have receded by 2000, they were still very present. For example, an advertisement in 2000 (p.1160) 'Laundry Centre. Complete washing and ironing centre. Features washing machine with opening door and pull and fold away ironing board' and also 'Hoover vacuum cleaner. Real vacuum cleaner function with remarkable dust container and polystyrene pellets to pick up.' The role of domestic chores was still very much marketed to girls.

Girls: Getting married

Another aspect associated with girls is the notion of getting married which is also reinforced by other media such as *Disney*. For example, in 1960 (p.702) a doll commercial noted: 'Here comes the Bride' and 'Miss Rosebud Bride doll... All 19 inches of her immaculately dressed for the great occasion... Rosebud teenage doll. Bridesmaid to the Bride doll.' This however, did wane slightly in different eras with the dolls becoming a little more independent. In 1967 (p.998) for example, Sindy has a boyfriend called Paul, a horse and her own car, although her outfits still include a 'long evening dress' because she still needs to look 'pretty.' Still popular in 1983 (p.948) Sindy not only has a horse and outfit to match but 'Sindy Pop Singer Doll wearing a polkadot dress with Black tights and fashionable headband. She has her own guitar and electronic organ. Complete with a party fun outfit of pink blouse and pantaloons' (1983: 948). Thus, it is still important for Sindy to be fashionable and to be aware of how she looks: 'Sindy Fashion Faces Doll. Dressed in a stunning white satin gown' (1983: 948). This is teaching girls that whilst the discourse of marriage and being a bride may have waned at times, there is still pressure on girls to find a male partner and to look good in order to attract a partner. The discourse of being a bride was still present with the Barbie doll in 2000 (p.1168) 'Princess Bride Barbie. Barbie wears a white chiffon dress with tiara and veil. Remove her blue bodice and transform her from a princess into a beautiful bride. When she raises her hand you can hear the music of true love.' This presents girls with stereotyped notions of being a 'princess' as well as being a future bride. The advertisement links these notions together – perhaps perpetuating the myth of a bride being a princess for the day. It also normalises marriage, weddings and romance as Ingraham (1999: 120 cited in Engstrom, 2011: 245) noted: 'Weddings, marriage, romance and heterosexuality become naturalised to the point where we consent to the belief that marriage is necessary to achieve a sense of well-being, belonging, passion, morality and love.' The advertisements in Kays Catalogue reinforce these notions for girls, who are taught that this is how they will find well-being and belonging.

Girls: Body Image

The discourses in Kays Catalogue teach girls how to do gender and particularly teach them how they should look. The focus on looks runs through the entire 80 years of the Catalogue. Even words associated with toys suggest that girls should be 'beautiful' and 'pretty.' For example: 'The Princess Betty. This is the favourite Baby Doll. Prettily dressed in her birthday party clothes of cream material' (1928: 220). This encourages girls to think they should also be pretty. Another advertisement in 1947 (p.86) highlighted 'A very chic little Doll, wearing a dainty floral flock with matching bonnet. She has lovely mid brown hair... one of the sweetest Dolls you can possess.' Being lovely and sweet is presented as suitable aspirations for girls. In 1960 (p.702) an advertisement highlighted: 'Denise pedigree doll. What an appealing look! Irresistible little doll neatly dressed in blue and white cotton print dress with lace trimmings, undergarment, socks and shoes.' This teaches a girl that being looked at is a norm for their gender. On the same page, another advertisement noted: 'As well dressed as a fashion model. Hat and coat in white printed chicken foot corded velvet worn over red/white cotton dress....nylons and high heeled shoe. To complete the ensemble: neat earrings.' These advertisements suggests that girls need to be appealing and should be concerned with being (or appearing) fashionable. This expanded to make-up for dolls in 1967 (p.999): 'Mary make-up. Tressy's best friend Mary loves to make-up and she comes complete with her make-up kit. She's a perfect fit for all Tressy's outfits. She is wearing a Jersey dress, pants, shoes and a hair band. Her make-up kit includes lipstick, eye shadow, nail polish and hair colouring.' This reinforces the idea that girls need to change themselves in order to look attractive and appealing. The notion of the use of make-up becoming the norm continued in 1983 (p.949) with a Sindy doll that came with a 'Beauty case contains three make-up pencils, cold cream make-up remover, two hair grips and slide.' In order to become beautiful, girls have to 'do' something which reinforces the script for being female. By 2000 (p.1165) the notion of make-up had extended to the female child being able to alter her own appearance along with the doll: 'A 50 cms doll with growing hair. You can change yours and the doll's hairstyle with the plaiting machine and other accessories. You can also change hair colour with the Blo pens and create your own design with the stencils. For use on the doll's or your own clothes (washing out in cold water).' The link between the doll and child is complete. Both need to change their appearance in order to fit into perceived gender appropriate norms.

Whilst the advertising of make-up is more obvious, the words such as pretty, looking irresistible and things to do with appearance are more subtle in relation to body image. The focus on how dolls should look is suggesting to girls that they should also focus on how they look. This theme is also present in relation to clothing for girls. For example, an advertisement for girl's clothing in 1920 (p.156) described the garment as 'dainty and useful' as well as 'here is one of the most charming pinafores we have ever produced.' These themes are repeated in 1930 (p.64): 'Give her dainty clothes and delight her little heart...Smart clothes to give charm and grace to the little toddler.' Being charming and graceful is something girls should aspire to. This continues with the comment: 'We think every small Girlie will look extremely pretty in this dress...it is a real beauty and will be admired wherever seen.' This reinforces the notion that girls are there to be looked at and admired. This continues throughout the life of the Catalogue. For example, in 1960 (p.101) 'Swagger coat high style for girls!...Coat is made even more attractive by using one of the season's most popular colour' (which was blue). The theme of looking pretty was constant throughout the life of the Catalogue. By 2000, there was some differentiation for girls in terms of clothing discourse: 'kit-teen for fresh and funky females (2000: 382) and 'combat dungarees' (2000: 448). Despite this there were still dresses such as 'Barbie Dress. Sparkly dress with round neck and badge' and 'Barbie Bikini. Sparkly Bikini' for ages 3-4, 5-6 and 7-8 years of age' (2000: 394). This is still teaching young girls how to perform their femininity.

Both the toy advertising and clothing advertising are suggesting to girls that how they look is vitally important. Being pretty and attractive is what girls should aspire to. Even in 2000, the discourse may cater for slightly different versions of femininity, but there is still the focus on appearance and being attractive. The make-up kits and other accessories that come with the dolls also teach girls that they need to change their appearance in order to look attractive. The importance of looks for girls underpins the advertisements throughout the 80 years of the Catalogue and is a powerful discourse that may influence girls in terms of gender and self-perception. Welch et al. (1979) suggest that it is the more subtle ideology that is less questioned and accepted. It is our contention that whilst advertising toys and clothing, the Catalogue has also been selling gendered discourses that require girls to conform to specific norms and expectations.

Discourses of gender: Boys

Boys, on the other hand, are not addressed in the same way as girls. Instead there are different themes that emerge. For boys, the advertisements convey a sense of adventure and excitement, as well as aggression and fighting. There is also a sense of future occupations highlighted in the toys and clothing commercials in the Catalogue.

Boys: Military/fighting

Boys are often shown playing with guns and fighting in many of the toy advertisements and this may aid the normalisation of aggression as a perceived masculine characteristic. MacKinnon (2003) has noted that the media often normalises this link and the Catalogue is therefore part of this wider discourse. Welch et al. (1979: 208) found that messages about what is masculine conveyed through television commercials included aggression. Our analysis of the advertising in Kays Catalogue suggests that this is also the case for advertisements aimed at boys. One of the first advertisements in 1939 (p.314) was for a 'Tommy Atkins Outfit. Complete set, comprising khaki coloured metal helmet, rifle and shooting corks, revolver, bandolier with ammunition in pockets. Just the set to delight the 'young soldier'.' Of course, 1939 is a significant date for such an outfit but this theme of aggression or violence continued throughout the life of the Catalogue. In 1953 (p.157) there was an advert: 'Space Shooting Range. An exciting game for the modern child. All metal range with moving space ship targets, powered by a long running clockwork mechanism with start and stop level. Complete with revolving gun and pellets.' Similarly in 1960 (p.732): 'Rustlers 45 Cap Pistol. Replica of the most famous Cowboy gun of the Wild West. Very strongly made and complete with six cap-loading bullets. Fully revolving chamber, spring loaded ejector and hinge-loading gate. Fast fanning action. Your boy will love these pistols.' This teaches boys that this is what they should be playing with and some boys may adapt to ensure their behaviour fits in with perceived gender appropriate behaviour (Mitra and Lewin-Jones, 2012).

The theme of guns and boys continued in 1977 (p.940): 'The Supersonic gun. Trigger action for Green, White and Red 'rays' plus high frequency buzz activated by independent switch.' Guns are also associated with the military in 1980 (p.938): 'Military truck. Featuring opening doors and hatch, removable canopy, drop down tailboard and swivel action machine gun' and in 2000 (p.1178) 'This missile firing vehicle can be used on land or in water.' This continuous theme of fighting and aggression could suggest to boys that aggression and violence is part of masculine behaviour. It may be the case that parents and peer groups may reinforce or challenge these gender stereotypes (Dyer, 1982) but Kays Catalogue provides a constant and stable discourse about boys in relation to fighting and aggression.[2] By contrast there was little or no aggression in the toys marketed to girls.

Boys: Action and fun

When toys are marketed at boys themes such as fun, adventure and being active are highlighted. For example, one commercial for a page of toys noted: 'Lots of fun for the boys' (1939: 134). The type of toys that are marketed includes such things as: 'Plastic train set. Just the toy a boy will welcome' (1947: 86). This ensures that boys know the train set is for them. Words such as 'fun' and 'exciting' tended to be used when advertising to boys. Similarly in 1967 (p.1020) another advertisement suggested: 'Be a real test driver. Johnny Speed. You drive it by remote control...you are in control all the way with Johnny Speed.' Thus the use of a male name ensures that boys know this is a toy they should want to play with. The idea of being active continued throughout the Catalogue. For example, in 1973 (p.996) there was a commercial for a jeep which was 'Just what a fellow needs to get from here to there in record time! Super strong, pedal propelled, with a plastic body that will not rust.' This suggests to the male child not only the kind of toy that he should be playing with but also how he should be actively playing. The theme of adventure is also highlighted in the Catalogue. For example, a 1977 (p.940) commercial highlighted: 'Adventure kit. Set contains: belt, utility pouch, binoculars, water flask with strap, compass, real camera, whistle and lanyard torch and adventure badge.' Adventure was highlighted as something that boys (but not girls) would be interested in. These tend to encourage the male child to be more active and to expect fun and to imagine themselves as adventurers and racing drivers rather than doing housework or looking after children.

Boys: Occupations

Kays Catalogue often noted particular occupations for boys which were different to those highlighted for girls. Other advertisements highlight the expected outdoors nature of boys such as: 'Giant tractor driven by strong clockwork spring

2. Hutchinson (2012) provides a very useful account of the way in which 'war-toys' and their consumption illustrated wider concerns about the consumption of toys by boys during the 1980s and the wider political concerns in which they were implicated.

in rear wheel' (1953: 156) and a 'David Brown Tractor by Sharna – a strong model pedal tractor... A child's model for the famous 'David Brown' farm tractor in authentic colours' (1973: 996). These advertisements suggested that such things as driving tractors was something that boys would do – linking physical exercise and activity as a norm for boys. There were also advertisements for carpentry sets: 'Wooden Tool Set. Beautifully presented carpentry set in wooden carrying case. Tools include fretsaw, hammer, vice, plane etc. Everything for the young carpenter' (1983: 970). Similarly in 1997 (p.1116) there was an '84 piece super work bench set with working vice, pretend saw, storage compartments, pretend nuts and bolts and electronic drill.' The carpenter theme continued into 2000 (p.1148) with 'Bear Carpenter. 28-piece tool centre for your little carpenter. Includes vice, play tools, lots of nuts, bolts and screws. Incorporates a handy storage compartment.' This was clearly something that is teaching boys that using tools involved in carpentry is something boys should do – and therefore links physical occupations (and perhaps DIY) as a way of performing masculinity.

Boys: Clothing

Whilst there were clear themes that came through the advertisements for clothing aimed at girls, there were less clear themes in the clothing aimed at boys. One theme however that did seem to be present was that of sports and the assumption that a boy will be playing sport. For example, 1940 (p.96) 'Like Father, like Son! The sports suit has earned its place amongst boys clothing outfits. More popular than ever. Sporting in appearance, light in weight, yet durable.' Whilst the theme of leisure and sport tended to be prominent, in the 80s branded sportswear was becoming promoted. For example, 1980 (p.395) 'Kevin Keegan Sportswear' and the Olympics were also mentioned: 'Olympic sweatshirt. Boy's long sleeve shirt with Moscow 1980 Olympic motif on front' (1980: 395). Similarly, rugby tops were advertised as everyday wear in later editions of the Catalogue. Thus there was an association with football and rugby as well as the professionalization of sports for boys.

Dressing up outfits: Boys and girls.

Some of the dressing up clothes for boys emphasised particular occupations, particularly when advertised by a male model. As well as this there were dressing up outfits linked to various occupations for boys. For example (1939: 314): 'This outfit includes smart conductor's peaked cap, number badge, money bag, with 50 passenger tickets, a three-way spring clip ticket holder and a bell ringing ticket punch' and just in case the children are unsure to whom this advertisement is aimed, it also suggests 'Lots of fun for the boys.' Another outfit is a 'Mobile Police set. Your boy will get hours of amusement with this outfit. Traffic Policeman 'G' Man or AA Patrol. Comprising Hat, Goggles, two white cuffs, notebook and pencil, pistol, belt, whistle and watch' (1939: 314). Similarly, in 1953 (p.156): 'Here's the outfit any 7 to 9 year old boy would love. Consisting of a felt halt... complete with Deputy Sheriff's badge. In 1980 (p.938) there was an 'Action Man Police Outfit. A complete uniform for motorcycle patrol duties.' So boys are taught that there are certain jobs that they should aspire to.

For girls, there were very different outfits which suggested different occupations. For example: 'Emergency Ward 10 Nurses Outfit. Official Uniform Headdress, pinafore, blue striped cotton dress and lined cape. Toy instruments include stethoscope, forceps, thermometer, syringe, watch etc. All in a carrying case' (1960: 732). Nursing was particularly focused on for girls as it is assumed that girls will have a nurturing, caring nature – thus suggesting these characteristics as the norm for girls. The other type of dressing up outfits for girls included such things as 'Barbie Dress. Sparkly dress, with round neck and badge' and 'Barbie Dress. Halter neck style, with embroidery to front chest and ties to back neck in towelling' (2000: 1146). This is in comparison to the different type of dressing up outfits for boys which included such things as Six Million Dollar Man outfit (1977: 940), or a Spiderman suit (1983: 968) and a racing drivers outfit (2000: 1146). By contrast the dressing up outfits for girls were more passive and less active compared with the male superheroes that tended to dominate the dressing up outfits for boys.

Gender: Toys for both boys and girls

In some editions of the Catalogue, the same toys were marketed to both girls and boys without being differentiated. For example: 'Wagon and bricks. Both the little girl and boy will be delighted with these brightly coloured bricks' (1932: 312). Where toys were concerned, the emphasis on the younger child was highlighted by words such as 'little'. Another example of a toy marketed at both boys and girls included: 'General stores. Kiddies just delight in playing at shops' (1947: 86) had 2 boys and 1 girl playing with the toy. For some things, this began to change slowly, when in 1953 (p.156) a tea set was coloured pink and clearly indicated as being for the female child. The colour blue was not yet associated as not being for girls, although pink was clearly a girl's colour. Similarly in 1980 (p.922) a china tea set was advertised as being 'for doll's tea parties' indicating that this was for girls rather than boys. There was no equivalent tea set marketed for boys. In 1973 a page spread with pedal cars had all male models indicating that these were intended for boys. However, in 1997 (p.1116) a 'mini chef kitchen centre. Features microwave with timer, bell, phone, oven with clicking ring, fridge with drinks dispenser, baby feeding seat, fold out table, storage and 16 cookware set' had both a young girl and boy playing with it. However, the fact it was called chef suggested that this was perceived as a profession rather than as a domestic chore. By 2000 (p. 1146) the pink and blue differentiation of the same toy was observed for a 'Police 6 Volt Ranger.' The toys that were marketed at both boys and girls were more the exception towards the end of the catalogue. The few toys that were marketed at both genders highlighted that these were for young children.

Gender: Clothes for both boys and girls.

In many editions of the Catalogue there were some clothes that were advertised for both boys and girls. For example, 1920 (p.160): 'Dainty coats for your little toddler. Suitable for chilly day wear. Suitable for either boy or girl.' Similarly in 1920 (p.158) 'child's frock overall, suitable for either boy or girl.' Many of these editions of the catalogue had black and white pictures of the clothing rather than colour. Later on, when colour was present in the catalogue, there were still some clothing marketed at both boys and girls. For example, in 1950 (p.5) there was 'Outerwear for girls and boys.' And this continued in the 1970s with (p.255) 'Boys/girls anorak....boys/ girls jeans in Navy cotton denim.' In 1980 there was a 'Boy/girl duffle coat' and 1990 (p.324-5) a 'Rugby top for boys and girls' as well as 'Comfort fit jeans for boys and girls.' Towards the end of the catalogue, the wording surrounding this advertisement highlighted the 'use value' rather than the symbolic value of clothing. It is far less likely that something advertised mainly at girls would also be marketed at boys, whereas there are some things marketed to boys are also marketed to girls. This reveals the hegemonic nature (Gill, 2007) of masculinity – even in advertising aimed at children in the Kays Catalogue.

Discussion

The thematic analysis of Kays Catalogue has demonstrated a very clear set of discourses pertaining to boys and girls: through the clothes that they are given to wear and the toys with which they are encouraged to play, the gender order is being presented and represented. What makes this analysis of the gendering of children through advertisements in Kays Catalogue all the more pertinent is the rise of the 'child as consumer' through much of the century. The gender order has been reinforced through the consumption practices of children or at least by their parents on their behalf.

Zelizer, in her now classic text *Pricing the Priceless Child,* argued that there was a profound transformation in the social value of children between 1870-1930, as a result of the creation of the US Labor Laws, whereby the 'twentieth-century economically useless but emotionally priceless child displaced the nineteenth-

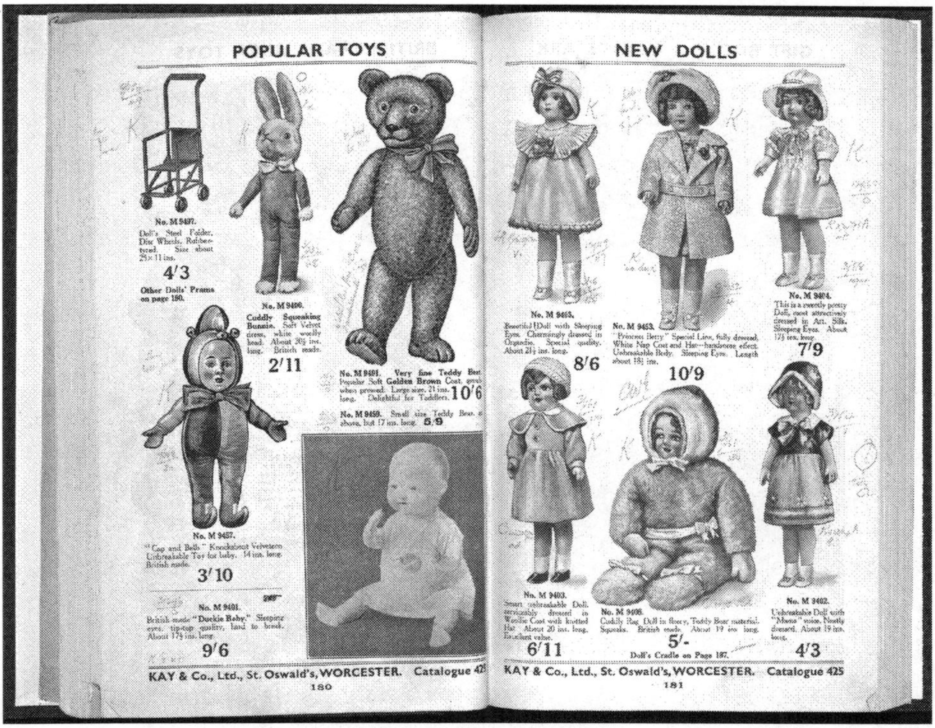

(Kays Catalogue, 1933: 180. Autumn and Winter)

century useful child' (1985: 209). The legislative changes as a result of the various Factory Acts during the nineteenth century and the Elementary Education Act 1870 in the UK would arguably have had a similar, if unintentional, effect.

We suggest that the increase in the number of pages devoted to the sale of toys and children's clothing as the century progressed (cf Coopey & Porter, 2003: 232), and also highlighted in other media, was reflective of the rise of 'the priceless child' but also in the changing relationship between child and parent, with parents living vicariously to some extent through their children and also reliving their own childhood.[3] Additionally, as Martens et al. (2004: 168) note: 'Children play a significant role in their parents' reflexive narration of self-identity and capacities to freely adopt different lifestyles or even multiple identities'. Thus the advertisements in Kays Catalogue become more significant when we consider the gender dimension in combination with the rise of the child as consumer and child as reflective of its parents.

If we accept the premise that once 'the child' has been constructed as economically useless and becomes something that parents could use to enjoy

3. See Cross (2004) for an analysis of advertisements in the US in the nineteenth and early twentieth centuries, and a demonstration of the interplay between children's consumption practices and their parents' expectations and behaviours around goods and play.

their childhood vicariously, it is also possible to note that the 'play' the parents engaged in, and therefore the toys they bought and consumed for and with their children, was gendered.[4] It is therefore not unsurprising that, as our analysis of the advertisements has shown, the toys were gendered and remain gendered, and this is something which has become more explicit as the century progressed (cf. Moorhead, 2007).

It has also been noted that there is a social class dimension to the consumption of Kays Catalogue (Casey, 2014; Clarke, 1998; Coopey & Porter, 2003) and therefore it is possible to suggest tentatively that the kind of toys and the clothing presented in the catalogues appeals to the gendered expectations and aspirations of a particular social class. For example, our earlier discussion of the occupations for boys as reflected in the toys with which they were encouraged to play are reflective of particular class-tendencies (working with a carpentry set or driving a tractor during the 1930s), although admittedly there are few toys which reflect middle-class boys' ultimate career destinations; equally telling are the toys for girls which focus on domestic labour such as cooking and cleaning. There is a tension here for a catalogue which promoted itself as 'aspirational'.[5]

So, following on from this, we would argue that the rise of the number and volume of advertisements aimed at children reflects the rise of the importance of child as consumer or children as a new market. From our analysis of the advertisements themselves we are able to identify clearly the gendered discourses which pervade the pages. Whether it is the child or the parent who acts as the driver of this consumption we are not able to comment upon. The wider literature, however, would suggest that the advertisements for children's toys and clothing appeal to the primary care-giver, usually women, as well as the child, and thus child and carer can be conceived of as co-consumers (Cook, 2008; Miller, 1997; Sparrman & Sandin, 2012). It is, as we discussed earlier, a means by which children (particularly younger children) and parents are reflective of each other in terms of (gender) identity in a multiplicity of ways.

This particular form of co-consumption, we would suggest, has lent itself to increasing gendered behaviour and more importantly, gendered expectations during the course of the twentieth century. It has been noted by Higonnet (1998) that almost half of all advertisement photographs show children and therefore we

---

4. We are careful not to assume that children, particularly older children, are mini-versions of their parents, or that their consumption patterns necessarily 'reflect their parents' material and social status' (Martens et al. 2004: 164). However, particularly whilst they are younger, there is necessarily a 'relationality' between the two in terms of their modes of consumption (Martens et al. 2004: 164) as parents 'not only act as gatekeepers regarding what can be consumed, but also actively engage in cultivating ways of consuming' (Martens et al. 2004: 166). This is then reflected in the types of toys and clothing made available for purchase via the Catalogue.
5. See Andrews (2015) for a discussion on the 'aspirational' nature of Kays catalogue.

should not be too surprised if the advertisements aimed at toys and clothing for children themselves, as illustrated by Kays Catalogue, become more gendered. Indeed as we have seen the discourses present very narrow stereotypical versions of gendered present and future selves through the type of clothing and toys advertised.

Conclusion

It was very clear from analysing Kays Catalogue (1920-2000) that there were clearly different discourses for boys and girls and that these discourses reinforced a binary notion of gender. In essence the advertisements (and catalogues themselves) demonstrate the notion, and process of, 'becoming' (see de Beauvoir, 2011; Butler, 1990).[6] From the toy advertisements in Kays Catalogue, we observed that the notion of becoming a mother and looking after a doll was only perceived as appropriate for girls, whereas boys were expected to be active, adventurous and associated with the military or fighting. Girls were associated with having to look a certain way such as being pretty whereas boys were associated with playing sports and having leisure time. The notion of housework persisted to 2000 for girls, with pink vacuum cleaner toys being marketed towards girls. The notion of getting married or finding a boyfriend was highlighted in the toys for girls whereas the converse did not feature in the toys for boys.

There were very different occupations highlighted in the advertisements for girls and boys. For example, for boys there were carpenter sets and diggers whereas for girls there were nurse outfits and associations of motherhood. Overall there appeared to be a wider variety of occupations suggested for boys compared with those for girls. Similarly, the clothing for boys did not focus on appearance whereas the clothing for girls specifically highlighted this aspect. Only a few toys were advertised as being for both boys and girls, but the main discourse that comes through the Catalogue is that girls and boys should perceive themselves as being different from each other. They should play with different toys and have different life expectations and occupations. Even in 2000 these were still the dominant discourses.

Whilst children may reject such notions (Repetti, 1984) it may be difficult if other media messages and peer groups also reinforce these ideas. For example, magazines, television and other media messages often have similar discourses and therefore normalise these messages. Similarly those who produce and market the goods reproduce the discourses of childhood (Pilcher, 2013) but as we are at pains to stress here, the combination of the advertisements used in the

6. See, for example, the discussion by Clarke (2007) of the use of more recent catalogues such as 'Party Pieces' to aid women in choosing the most socially appropriate items for their children's birthday parties.

media and the choice of goods offered, (re)create the gendered child as well as the gendered consumer.

Whilst we expected much to have changed from 1920 to 2000, there was actually very little change in the gendered discourses for toys and little change in the way that boys and girls were addressed through advertising. In fact, if anything, by 2000 the gender binaries were even more explicit in some cases than they were in the 1920s. This, as we have argued, also reflects the parallel rise of consumer culture and the notion of a particular kind of childhood during the late nineteenth and twentieth centuries, which at one level allowed for a modification of the representation of gender whilst simultaneously reinforcing the gender order through the discourses presented. Thus following Cook (2012: 55), Pilcher (2013), Rose (2013) and Sparrman and Sandin (2012) we would argue that the advertisements considered here allow us to move beyond seeking a singular account of that which is observed, and instead allow for a more complex picture to emerge which suggest that there are a number of 'values' in conversation with each other, which have had a gendering effect. The category of gender, as presented within these discourses, is somewhat surprising, and illustrates the complex multi-dimensional relationship between gender, childhood, and the rise of consumer culture during the twentieth century.

References

Andrews, M. (2015) Shopping for Identities and Purchasing Fantasies of Domesticity in Post-War Kays Catalogues In B.Mitra & R. Johnson (eds.) *Gender Construction in Kays Catalogues: 1920 to the New Millennium*, Cambridge, Cambridge Academic Ltd.
Aries, P. (1962) *Centuries of Childhood: A social history of family life*. New York: Vintage.
Braun, V. and Clarke, V. (2006) Using thematic Analysis in Psychology. *Qualitative Research in Psychology.* Vol. 3, pp. 77-101.
Buckingham, D. (2007) Selling Childhood? Children and Consumer Culture. *Journal of Children and Media.* Vol. 1(1), pp.15-24.
Buckingham, D. and Scanlon, M. (2001) Parental pedagogies: An analysis of British 'edutainment' magazines for young children. *Journal of Early Childhood Literacy.* Vol. 1(3), pp.281-299.
Butler, J. (1990) *Gender Trouble.* Oxon, Routledge.
Casey, E. (2014) Catalogue Communities: Work and consumption in the UK catalogue industry. *Journal of Consumer Culture.* http://joc.sagepub.com/content/early/2014/03/27/469540514528199.refs.html
Clarke, A. (2007) Making Sameness: Mothering, Commerce and the Culture of Children's Birthday Parties in E. Casey & L. Martens (eds.) *Gender and Consumption*, Aldershot: Ashgate
Cook, D. T. (2012) Pricing the Priceless Child – a wonderful problematic in A. Sparrman, B. Sandin & J. Sjoberg (eds.) *Situating Child Consumption.* Lund: Nordic Academic Press
Cook, D. T. (2008) The Missing Child in Consumption Theory. *Journal of Consumer Culture.* Vol. 8(2), pp. 219-243
Cook, D. T. (2004) *The Commodification of Childhood: The children's clothing industry and the rise of the child consumer.* Durham, NC: Duke University Press.
Coopey, R. & Porter, D. (2003) Agency Mail order in Britain c. 1900-2000: Spare-time agents and their customers in J. Benson & L. Ugolini (eds.) *A Nation of Shopkeepers: Five centuries of British retailing.* London: I B Tauris & Co.
Cross, G. (2004) *The Cute and the Cool: Wondrous Innocence and Modern American Children's Culture.* New York: Oxford University Press.
De Beauvoir, S. (2011) *The Works of Simone de Beauvoir.* Nook E-book, zuubooks.com.
Dyer, R. (1982) *Advertising as Communication.* New York, Methuen.
Engstrom, E. (2011) Unravelling the Knot: Political Economy and Cultural Hegemony in Wedding Media, in G. Dines and J.M. Humez (eds.) *Gender, Race*

and Class in Media. A Critical Reader. London, Sage.
Entwistle, J. (2000) *The Fashioned Body: Fashion, dress and social theory.* Cambridge: Polity Press.
Fielden, A.L., Sillence, E. and Little, L. (2011) Children's understandings of obesity, a thematic analysis. *International Journal of Qualitative Studies. Health and Well Being.* Vol. 6, pp.1-14.
Fowles, J. (1996) *Advertising and Popular Culture.* Thousand Oaks CA, Sage.
Garfinkel, H. (1967) *Studies in Ethnomethodology.* Upper Saddle River, N.J. Prentice Hall.
Gill, R. (2007) *Gender and the Media.* Cambridge, Polity.
Higonnet, A. (1998) *Pictures of Innocence: The history and crisis of ideal childhood.* London: Thames and Hudson.
Hutchinson, B.P.L. (2012) 'The Littlest Arms Race?': War toys and the boy consumer in Eighties' Canada in A. Sparrman, B. Sandin & J. Sjoberg (eds.) *Situating Child Consumption.* Lund: Nordic Academic Press.
Johnson, F.L. and Young, K. (2002) Gendered voices in children's television. *Critical Studies in Mass Communication.* Vol. 19(4), pp. 461-480.
James, A., Jenks, C. & Prout, A. (1998) *Theorizing Childhood.* New York: Teacher's College Press.
Lawlor, M.A. (2011) Pester Power – A battle of wills between children and their parents. *Journal of Marketing Management.* Vol. 27(5-6), pp.561-581.
MacKinnon, K. (2003) *Representing Men. Maleness and Masculinity in the Media.* London, Arnold.
Manstead, A. S. R and McCulloch, C. (1981) Sex-Role Stereotyping in British Television Advertisements. *British Journal of Social Psychology.* Vol. 20, pp.171-180.
Martens, L., Southerton, D. & Scott, S. (2004) Bringing Children (and Parents) into the Sociology of Consumption: Towards a theoretical and empirical agenda. *Journal of Consumer Culture.* Vol. 4(2): 155-182.
Mayne, I. (2000) The Inescapable images. Gender and Advertising. *Equal Opportunities International.* Vol. 19(2/3/4), pp. 56-61.
Milestone, K. and Meyer, A. (2012) *Gender & Popular Culture.* Cambridge, Polity.
Miller, D. (1997) Consumption and its Consequences in H. Mackay (ed.) *Consumption and Everyday Life.* Milton Keynes: Open University.
Mitra, B. and Lewin-Jones, J. (2012) Colin won't drink out of a pink cup. K. Ross (ed.) *Blackwell Handbook of Gender, Sexualities and the Media.* Oxford, Wiley-Blackwell, pp.383-400.
Moorhead, J. (2007) Girls will be Boys: Reading B in S. Bragg & MJ Kehily

(eds.) *Children and Young People's Cultural Worlds:* 2nd Edition. Bristol: Policy Press.

Pilcher, J. (2013) 'Small but Very Determined': A novel theorization of children's consumption of clothing, *Cultural Sociology*. Vol. 7(1): 86-100.

Repetti, R. L. (1984) Determinants of children's sex stereotyping: Parental sex-role traits and television viewing. *Personality and Social Psychology Bulletin.* Vol. 10(3), pp.457-468.

Rose, C. (2013) Maternal Consumption: A view from the past. *Journal of Consumer Culture.* Vol. 13(2), pp. 178-198.

Ross, J.A. and Green, C. (2011) Inside the experience of anorexia nervosa: A narrative thematic analysis. *Counselling and Psychotherapy Research.* June Vol. 11(2), pp. 112-119.

Russell, R. & Tyler, M. (2002) 'Girl Heaven' and the Commercial Context of Feminine Childhood. *Sociology*. Vol. 36 (3), pp. 619-637.

Sparrman, A. & Sandin, B. (2012) Situated Child Consumption in A. Sparrman, B. Sandin & J. Sjoberg (eds.) *Situating Child Consumption.* Lund: Nordic Academic Press.

Verna, M.E. (1975) The Female Image in Children's TV Commercials. *Journal of Broadcasting.* Vol. 19(3), pp.301-9.

Welch, R., Huston-Stein, A., Wright, J.C. and Plehal, R. (1979) Subtle sex-role cues in children's commercials. *Journal of Communication.* Vol. 29(3), pp.202-9.

Zelizer, V. (1985) *Pricing the Priceless Child: the changing social value of children.* New York: Basic Books.

// Chapter 2 //

The Construction of feminine and masculine gender identities through Advertising in Kays Catalogue (1920-2000)

Mehreen Mirza and Barbara M. Mitra

Introduction

Advertising is an integral part of contemporary society: all pervasive and everywhere, it is hard to escape the messages that are portrayed in advertising. It is partly through these messages that we learn what is acceptable and appropriate including perceived gender behaviour (Koll-Stobbe, 1994: 385). Advertising is text that is heavily gendered in the way it addresses its audience (Hodge and Kress, 1988: 66 cited in Matheson, 2005: 52). The messages that are portrayed in advertising tend to be fairly consistent in how they represent men and women such as 'slim beautiful people' (Mayne, 2000: 57) for women and the 'emphasis on the 'fit' male body' for men (Wykes and Gunter, 2005: 205). Since the late nineteenth-century mail-order, in its broadest sense, has carried meanings and purpose beyond a simple display of goods (cf. Schorman, 2003). Indeed, McCracken suggests that 'Great catalogues make meanings so powerfully that it is not unusual to hear consumers say that "they want to live in the catalogue"' (2005: 18). Thus, advertisements are texts that we can study in relation to discourses that are promoted through the commercials. Kays Catalogue provides us with an 80 year time period to study these discourses in relation to gender.

Discourses and Gender

There are specific discourses of masculinity and femininity which are presented through the media, of which advertising plays a powerful role (Koll-Stobbe, 1994: 385). There are specific discourses in relation to gender that appear to have changed little over time. For example, the notion of women conforming to a slender beauty image and having to look 'young, slender, sexual and white' persists (Wykes and Gunter, 2005: 206). Men tend to be represented in relation to women (Matheson, 2005: 80). This relational categorisation of masculinity and femininity tends to highlight masculinities around 'violence, sporting prowess and the need to be intensely competitive' (Martin and Muthukrishna, 2011: 3805) compared with women who are presented as being 'quiet, gentle and ladylike, wearing the correct clothes' (Martin and Muthurkrishna, 2011: 3802).

In most media, advertising included, 'Men act and women appear. Men look at women, women watch themselves being looked at' (Berger, 1972: 47 cited in Matheson, 2005: 80).

The discourses surrounding clothing advertising reproduce discourses of gender symbolically. Lazaroiu (2012: 163) suggests that 'fashion helps to reproduce gender as a form of body style.' Even though gender roles in society may have changed, the marketplace continues to perpetuate more traditional gender stereotypes (Hourigan and Bougoure, 2012: 129). Thus, despite Crane (2012: 20) suggesting that changes in social relations are replicated in clothing styles, we argue that advertising is very slow to reflect such changes. In this Chapter we have analysed whether there were dominant masculinities and femininities promoted through clothing advertising, using the Kays Catalogue to examine 80 years of advertisements. Our analysis of advertising necessarily includes a consideration of the way in which patterns of consumption occur through Kays Catalogue, thus enabling us to consider how advertising, consumption and gender intertwine to generate particular discourses around masculinity and femininity. Indeed Ugolini states in her work that advertisements should be 'considered in their role as intermediaries between the retailer and the potential purchaser, as a "common sartorial language" that encouraged and justified male [and female] consumption' (2003: 80-1).

Method

A pilot was conducted to establish whether there were sufficient clothing advertisements tagged with the terms 'Men' and 'Women.' Using the search engine on the World of Kays Website (http://www.worldofkays.org/) we explored the number of digital pages available for clothing advertisements aimed at men and women in different years. As there were numerous clothing commercials available for analysis, it was decided that capturing examples from every decade would give an insight to the discourse of gender in the catalogue. From 1920 to the Catalogue's demise in 2000, we captured clothing advertisements aimed at women and men. All clothing was included except for nightwear and underwear. In total 9 years were analysed which generated 203 clothing advertisements (133 relating to women and 70 to men).

The words surrounding the advertisements were transcribed to enable further analysis. Thematic analysis was used to analyse the material because of its 'accessible and flexible approach' (Griffiths et al, 2011: 169) in examining data. Thematic analysis involves 'the searching across a data set....to find repeated patterns of meaning (Braun and Clarke, 2006: 86). The transcribed material was read and re-read in order to explore themes in the data (Ross and Green,

2011: 113). We were guided by looking for themes that related to gender as we particularly wanted to explore whether there were persistent discourses in relation to masculinity (or masculinities) and femininity (or femininities). We also wanted to compare the relational nature of the discourses in the advertisements. The next section highlights the themes that emerged, focusing firstly on discourses of women in the advertisements.

Women: Being Pretty, Attractive and Beautiful

Throughout the 80 years of the archive, the theme of being pretty, attractive and beautiful dominated clothing advertising for women. For example, in 1920 (p.129) an advertisement for a 'Lady's Dainty Costume. Suitable for all occasions.' suggests that women should think of themselves as 'dainty' and associates this as being a feminine characteristic. Similarly in 1930 (p.106) another commercial noted a dress that was 'Tailored on the free hip principle that gives the graceful movement from waist downwards and promotes an attractive fashionable line.' The correlation between attractiveness and grace freighted through clothing is clearly an aspirational theme here. The onus on being attractive also continued in an advert from 1940 (p.5) 'We vote this one of the most charming little frocks we've seen for several seasons! Note the attractive cowl neck-line, the cleverly cross-cut bodice which gives such a flattering fit.' In 1950 (p.19) an advertisement links beauty with elegance for women when promoting 'A smart and original two-piece of elegantly tailored beauty.' This perhaps suggests that women themselves can be fashioned into becoming beautiful and that the clothing is a part of this process. Part of being pretty and attractive is also associated with being feminine: 'Adorably feminine. A beautiful party dress in soft-toned nylon flocked with dainty flowers. Sleeveless with a flattering roll collar' (1960: 148). Thus for women being feminine is to be adorable, beautiful, dainty and attractive. Even in 2000 the theme of being attractive and beautiful was still very present. For example, a 'Long sleeved cardigan' is 'Beautifully embroidered with trim edging.' (2000: 278). Although the words are describing the clothing, the advertisements are, we would suggest, in reality describing the women and suggesting how they should view themselves.

Women: Being Looked At

The discourse of being looked at is one that appears in many different media forms, and it is one that is also present in the clothing advertising aimed at women in Kays Catalogue. The advertisements in the Catalogue promote the notion that women want to be looked at, and found attractive, by men. Sometimes men are shown in the advertisements for female clothing. This discourse can be found in 1920 (p.134): 'You will be delightful with this up-to date model, which fastens down the side. Front panel fitted with dainty little patch pockets with button decorations.' This does not suggest that they will be delighted but that they themselves should become delightful and therefore looked at and admired. Similarly in 1940 (p.5) a feature intoned: 'One in a Million. A Two-piece that you'll wear whenever you want to look your charming best' therefore looking good and being charming is a discourse that does tend to dominate. The notion of looking good at work was also highlighted in 1960 (p.74) 'You feel better... you work better...when you know you look better! ... Bib apron in attractive contemporary print cotton with wide halter neck in contrast colour to match pocket.' Thus, for women how they look actually feeds into both self-esteem and their perceived productivity, be they engaged in paid or unpaid labour.

In 1970 (p.294) the 'Birds of Britain' advertisements featuring clothing for women: 'As Britain leads the world in Motor Racing, the 'Birds of Britain' Fashion House leads the world in clothes design.' This reinforced the theme of women being valued for how they look rather than what they might do. This particular set of advertisements draws on the (sexist) language of the time which regularly referred to women as 'birds' as in 'Tune up *British Birds* and get into harmony with the 'BIRDS OF BRITIAN' Fashion House ...' (1970: 294, our emphasis).[1] Such language clearly pervaded the Catalogue and the narratives employed to locate and promote its products. In 1980 the notion of being looked at was emphasised by the use of being 'alluring': 'Single Shoulder Maxi Dress, Sizzling with Style! Super diamante shoulder strap, charming ruching, alluring side slit and unmistakable elegance are sure to attract admiring glances.' These admiring glances are from men who do the looking. Men are active and women are passive in the same way that Mulvey (1989) highlighted in relation to film. Indeed Crane and Bovone (2006: 232) comment that 'photographs of women in fashion magazines are constructed as if they were intended for the young male spectator's gaze and embody his expectation of women and of male-female relationships'. This theme is emphasised in an advertisement from 2000 (p.1) which described a: 'soft, elegant style [...] ideal when you want to dress to impress.' These discourses then, normalise the notion of women as passive (being looked at) and men as active (doing the looking).

---

1. The review of the London fashion scene during the 1960s to the early 1970s by the Victoria and Albert Museum discusses the kind of women to whom various types of on-trend clothing would appeal. With reference to the Biba store (run by Barbara Hulanicki), they draw on a quotation from *Time* magazine which stated that Biba was 'The most "in" shop for gear ... A must scene for the switched on dolly bird' (April 1966) http://www.vam.ac.uk/content/articles/f/1960s-fashion-london/ (our emphasis). Similarly, the book, 'Birds of Britain' was produced by the photographer John Green which showcased British models and actresses of the 1960s. The language used to describe (young) women in these articles and the Catalogue is clearly reflective of the time.

(Kays Catalogue, 1950: 64, Spring and Summer)

Women: Being Thin

Another theme that is part of this notion of body image and being looked at is the idea of being thin (Wykes and Gunter, 2005). This is present from around the 1940s onwards as being both appropriate and desirable for women. In 1940 (p.13) one advertisement promoted 'Young fashions designed to keep you looking slim and smart.' A decade later, the Catalogue advertised 'Slenderizing models for fuller figures...A practical frock, specially designed to tone down the fuller figure and ease inches off the width' (1950, p.17) so here the clothing helps make the customer appear slim and fuels the desire to appear slim. Of course, if this was not possible, then one can always cover up: 'Clever you! To choose this slimming cardigan jacket' (1960: 70). Advertisements in the 1970s also highlighted this discourse such as (1970: 84) 'Two-tone dress. A Clifton Slimline dress showing off the pinafore look in Briar with classically contrasting Ecru for the short sleeves and inset yoke.' Calling the dress slimline is itself symbolic of slimness promoted as being desirable. Similarly in 1980 (p.122-3) Kays featured a 'Special cut. Look Slimmer' style and a 'Dress and jacket. Flattering silky polyester dress in a delightful floral print.' Here the emphasis on achieving a slim look is a continuous discourse, reinforced by the kind of women used in the advertisements themselves (cf. Redmond, 2003). By the 1990s consumers were being advised to cover up if they were not slim. 'The softer style of denim, teamed with feminine embroidered tips. Note the flattering length of the cover-up cardigan' (1990: 274). This suggests that femininity is not merely associated with classic feminine tropes such as 'softness', but also with conforming to a certain body shape. This was stressed in 2000 (p.279) where 'Slima co-ordinating separates' and 'Clip 'n' slide expandable waist for extra comfort' were advertised. Thus, not only are women used to being looked at but the notion of having to look slim is also reinforced through the discourses in the advertisements. So we note here a contradiction: a recognition that the women who buy from the Catalogue do not meet the exacting standards of beauty and size promoted by wider society and the Catalogue itself and therefore products need to be supplied which accommodate women's actual body shape, whilst simultaneously reinforcing the notion that the women need to conform as best they can and, if they cannot, they ought to 'cover up'. This would suggest a superficial conforming, but a conforming nonetheless in an ego-ideal relationship (Laplanche and Pontalis, 2006). As we shall see later in this chapter, men are addressed by advertising in the Catalogue in a very different way.

Women: Occupations

The kind of occupations that are promoted through the advertising in the Catalogue tend to suggest the perceived appropriate occupations for women at the time, and are reflective of the working-class nature of the consumer base of the Catalogue (cf. Andrews, 2015; Casey, 2014; Clarke, 1998; Clarke, 2007; Coopey & Porter, 2003; Coopey et al, 2005). For example: 'The Universal Apron. The nursing profession speak in glowing terms of this particular production. Most serviceable to the lady or maid who requires a really tough wearer. Its wearing qualities cannot be equalled...Maids smart apron with embroidered bib and long shoulder straps' (1930: 117). Thus in 1930s being a nurse or maid was considered an entirely appropriate occupation for the Catalogue's customer base. This continued into the 1940s (p.52) where 'Housemaid's dresses, aprons and caps' and 'Nurse's or Maid's Morning Apron in White Croydon. Unsurpassed for wear' were extensively advertised. In 1940 (p.10) it was also acknowledged that women were working in various office-based environments with Kays promoting 'Business wear...you buy smartness here'; this implies that women needed to acquire smartness rather than this being an innate attribute for women. There were a few different occupations mentioned in 1970. For example, a 'Short-sleeved drill overall' was marketed as 'Ideal for shop assistants, chemists etc ... Gives all over protection.' Despite this, the dominant occupation in relation to clothing is that of being a housewife, homemaker and mother, and this is reflected in the general perception of the aspirations of women during much of the twentieth century (cf. Andrews, 2015). Within this model of perceptions, women were firmly associated within the domestic arena of the home. For example, in 1970 (p.100-1) Kays promoted a 'Cover up story... on the kitchen scene... Apron and oven mitts...a useful set in printed cotton travelling. The lined mitts can be attached to the apron by means of Velcro strips at each wrist.' In 1980 (p.58) Kays advertised a 'Housedress. Short sleeved button thro' style with concealed pockets', thereby continuing to reinforce the idea of domesticity and domestic labour as appropriate for women. Indeed, this is a trend that is evident throughout the life of the Catalogue: Coopey et al. (2005: 100) suggest that from the 1930s onwards the Catalogue advised 'women on the art of being a housewife and caring for the family'.

As suggested earlier there are some advertisements which highlighted the field of business as an appropriate occupation for women. This occurs in 1990 where the language of corporate advancement – a leitmotif of the age – was increasingly employed. Thus, women could access: 'Working capital that shows you mean business' (1990: 22). Similarly in 2000 (p.10) Kays offered a 'Working wardrobe. Make an impression wherever you work with a look that's as stylish as it is smart.' This suggests that there is recognition that more occupations were open to women by 2000, but that it was (and is still) more important how a woman looks.

One occupation that remained stable throughout the 80 years was that of being a mother or anticipating becoming a mother. One would expect this in the early editions of the Catalogue such as in 1930 (p.20) where a 'Pleasing Model for Mother's wear.' was noted. However, this theme was still present in later editions of the Catalogue. In 1970 (p.234) 'The waiting game. Maternity wear' suggests that pregnancy is an expected stage of life and therefore motherhood is natural role for women. Similarly, another advertisement in 1970 (p.220) headed 'Baby Days', identified a range of 'Maternity wear to make you look your best while playing "The Waiting Game"'. By 2000 the conception of motherhood had moved from being a passive anticipatory stage of life to one which was active, albeit in relation to the raising of children. Kays naturally provided the requisite clothing and accessories: 'Fun day out. If you're out and about with the kids you'll need a little casual style – and plenty of practical extras like this fashionable bag'.

The variety of roles for women and the construction of feminine identities displayed in the advertisements over the life of the Catalogue show the tension that existed between offering women identities which reflected the work/roles that they already do, and the work/roles that they might want to do. It is the tension between the real-world and the dream-world of the Catalogue. Crane (2000: 18) suggests that 'choices of consumer goods [for women] become a complex form of negotiation between conflicting hegemonic norms, conveyed through images in the media, and her own understanding of gender differences'. Moreover, Crane argues that clothing and its uses, which here we argue is manifested through advertising, 'is always socially motivated' (2000: 19): it reflects and refracts the changes in the social roles of women, whilst also still rooting the women and their gender identities in their particular social space. Consumption is available to all but we do not all consume equally. The next section focuses on discourses of masculinity in Kays Catalogue.

Men: Occupations

One theme that was dominant for men throughout the 80 years of the Catalogue was that advertising was tied to specific suggested occupations for men, which, as noted earlier in relation to women were often class-specific (Casey, 2014; Clarke, 2007; Coopey and Porter, 2003; Coopey et al, 2005). The advertisements for men's clothing reflected a wider variety of jobs and occupations than did the clothing for women. For example, in 1930 (p.155) Kays featured: 'Men's shirts. Everyday wear shirts for the Bread Winner. The Harvard. This is a shirt generally worn during the summer months by the Artisan class.' During the earlier editions it was assumed that men were the breadwinners. This commercial also suggests that the target audience want to aspire to the 'Artisan' or a higher class through wearing a shirt that has those class associations. According to Miller (1991: 136) one way that people in lower classes emulate those in higher classes is by imitating or appropriating their clothing. Even so, Kays aimed squarely at the working-class purchaser. In 1939 (p. 149) it advertised 'Splendid value in Workman's overalls. Suitable for Engineers, Mechanics and All Allied Trades. Most of the goods in this class are chemically filled - ours are solid throughout.' So trades such as mechanics and engineers are seen as suitable male occupations. Other physically demanding manual trades were clearly core business as highlighted in an advertisement in 1950 (p.129) 'Bib and Brace overalls. Ideal for the mechanic etc. Strongly made in high grade Navy Twill'. Electricians also figure: 'Extra strong navy jacket. Ideal for mechanics, electricians...All seams are double sewn to ensure longer wear' (1950: 129). Warehouse workers and workshops also appear: 'Men's Drill Overcoat. Ideal for warehouse and workshop - gives complete protection. Cut from hard-wearing drill' (1960: 254). By 1970, the type of occupation had expanded to include: 'Practical protection for painters and decorators.... Lybo bib/brace overalls for painters and decorators, made to stand up to really rugged wear.' Thus, the type of appropriate occupations are assumed to be laborious and physically taxing. As opportunities opened up for men in the service industries alongside, as well as or instead of, more traditional working class occupations (cf. Fletcher, 2010), the advertising in the Catalogue became less specific and focused on the intrinsic value of the items. In 1980 'working jeans' were described in a non-occupationally specific way, simply described as having 'treble stitched seams' (p.464). In contrast, the word 'city' became associated with occupations for men: 'New approaches to classic casuals...new styles in city suits' (1990: 432). This position assumes that more men will be in urban, white-collar occupations which require suits rather than the hard wearing material of traditional, manual employment, and again reflects the rise of men in white-collar occupations (Collinson and Hearn, 2001). The consumption of clothing therefore acts as an indicator of aspirations for both men and women (McCracken, 2005), and yet at the same time Catalogues such as Kays have a democratizing effect – everything is within reach, so long as lines of credit are available (cf. Casey, 2014; Coopey et al, 2005).

Despite this implicit aspiration, there has always been the assumption that suits are also appropriate and necessary for men (cf. Ugolini, 2007; Schorman, 2003). So alongside the notion of a physically active working man, there is the notion of a gentleman in a suit. This again reflects the aspirational nature of the Catalogue (cf. Andrews, 2015; Coopey et al, 2005). The focus on suits is an interesting one, and reflective of the wider trend in advertisements in mail order shopping, especially when the claim is made that men were not as interested in shopping per se, and the data available repeatedly shows that the consumers of Kays Catalogue were primarily working-class women (cf. Andrews, 2015; Casey, 2014; Coopey et al, 2005). Nonetheless, we can draw on the work of Ugolini who comments that, 'In the case of men's clothing, therefore the commodity was not left to speak for itself, but acquired its significance and appeal [...] when it was associated with male identities and lifestyles that can be best described as "gentlemanly"' (2003: 86). Moreover, there is a clear indication of the advertisements reflecting a greater concern with the "modern"-facing world of the twentieth century (cf. Ugolini, 2003: 87).

Sometimes the clothing that was advertised was described as formal wear and smart. For example (1940: 101): 'Formal wear for the smart man [offered] Excellent wearing quality.' The notion of being stylish also came through the advertising: 'Lybro 'corporate' suit is the latest protective gear – a stylish worksuit in Green easy-care Terylene Cotton material' (1970: 432). The advertisements here offer its working-class clientele an opportunity to acquire (and reflect) a different kind of masculine role, the corporate office-worker, whilst simultaneously underscoring the lack of social status through the emphasis on its "easy-care" nature rather than the quality of its material. The 'democratization' of fashion during the course of the twentieth-century may seem to have blurred the boundaries between the social classes, as reflected during the life of the Catalogue, but in the end it can be seen that it is a somewhat superficial democratization as social status is increasingly marked out by small details, one of which is the 'quality' of the fabric used. Indeed, Entwistle argues:

> [T]he upper-class notion of 'quality and not quantity' will be reflected not only in decisions about the amount spent on individual items, but on the fabrics chosen (for example, silk, linen and cashmere as opposed to their synthetic substitutes). The predisposition to certain kinds of fabric and the notion of "quality" may be explained in the notion of "cultural capital" (2000: 51).

Clarke and Miller (n.d.) in their research note that their middle-class respondents used catalogues such as Land's End and Racing Green 'both of which promote the use of natural fibres and neutral colours and styles'. This stands in sharp contrast to the advertisements in Kays Catalogue which, as we have seen, focus on attributes related to the hard-wearing and synthetic or treated nature of the fabric.

Here, too, as with the clothing advertised for women, there is a clear tension between the reality of masculine identities available to the male consumers of Kays Catalogue and those that were available through the dream-world of the catalogue.

We would suggest that a range of masculine occupational identities are conveyed through the advertisements, from the manual worker through to the lower levels of white-collar work. We would, however, following Ugolini suggest that it is not a simple emulation 'or a desire to ape the fashions of those higher in the social hierarchy' (2003: 92). Indeed the emphasis on the rugged nature of the *work*-clothing stands contra to this general claim. However, there is a change in the Kays Catalogue as the century progresses where much of the clothing advertising discussed does 'embod[y] a lifestyle of luxury and pleasure, a lifestyle clearly available only to a minority of the male population' (Ugolini, 2003: 92), but it cannot be denied that the advertisements still emphasise the utility-value of the clothing.

The discourse is slightly different compared with the suits advertised for women. Instead of suggesting that they will *become* smart, it suggests that they *are* smart. Therefore the men are addressed as being smart rather than having to become smart. This is the core difference then - women are encouraged to judge themselves by what others think and perceive, whilst men are encouraged to think of themselves as an individual without looking to others for affirmation.

Men: Leisure and Sport

One theme that was apparent for men throughout the 80 years was that of being outdoors and being physically active, particularly with regards to sports. For example, in 1930 (p.140) an advertisement noted: 'Sports coat. The 'K' Sports Coat. If it is freedom, ease and comfort you are considering, then let us recommend new model sports Coat... Combining movement with stylish appearance.' Similarly in 1930 (p.152-3) Kays recommended 'Motor clothing. Leather Motor Coat Department. The Leader' and 'Gents motoring outfit in Double texture.' Sport, in particular, is perceived of as a characteristic of masculinity as highlighted by MacKinnon (2003: 102) who explored the 'well-attested links between maleness and sports.' The notion of being a sportsman figures in advertising of clothing for men. 'Men's sports shirts. Styled for coolness and comfort ... the ideal shirt for freedom loving Sportsman. Collar attached shirts in grey Ceylonetted, well suited to the outdoor man and admirable as an all-purpose shirt at all times of the year' (1950: 134). The sportsman is one appropriate version of masculinity on offer through the Catalogue. The idea of male bonding through sport is also highlighted in an advertisement: 'For outdoor occasions... protection and style. The latest in-look for modern men and their mates!' (1970: 414). There was also a greater variety of sports and sportswear, such as 'Golf overtrousers' and 'sailing trousers' available for men than for women. Similarly, the notion that men might want to engage with country activities and perhaps, therefore, associate with a perceived higher class is also evident. For example, in an advertisement in 1960 (p.2111) Kays presented a 'Cherwell semi-hacking sports jacket' and 'Sportsown plain lounge style sports jacket tailored from 61% Wool and 39% Pure Silk. Fashionable jetted side pockets.' There was also the 'Sportsown Gabardine golf jacket, specially designed to appeal to the golfer but also suitable for other sportswear' and 'A jacket that would be ideal for rambling, climbing and other outdoor pursuits' (1960: 224). Cricket was also mentioned in 1970 (p.437) 'Cricket sweater knitted in heavy cable stitch... the ideal wear for all sports.' Thus the range of sports highlighted by the advertising as suitable for men is more diverse than the sports highlighted for women.

The sport of rugby also figured in later editions of the Catalogue: 'Rugby shirts in a choice of 2 shirts and 3 colours' (1990: 471). There were also more brand names or sports names endorsing clothing in the 80s and up to 2000. For example in 1990 (p.486) a 'Ski Jacket by Trespass' and 'Slazenger Leisure wear approved by Ballesteros' appeared in the Catalogue. Names such as Adidas and Le Coq Sportif figured an 'Overhead jacket by Le Coq Sportif...The biggest names in sport and leisure, the hot new contenders and low cost essentials you can't afford to miss... On your marks, get set...Go!' (2000: 578). Thus, men are addressed as being much more physically active than women. They also tended to have more celebrity male role models to endorse these sports as being suitable, thus the meaning-transfer process cannot be denied (McCracken, 2005: 103-110).

Men: Weight

The issue of weight is treated very differently for men compared with women. Instead of focusing on covering up and being slim, it is not considered an issue at all. For example, 1940 (p.96) 'Lined hard wearing Italian. Trousers are made like ordinary 'flannels' with extension waist-band, belt loops and adjusting straps.' The provision of clothing with extension waistbands continued in other advertisements in a matter of fact way. The words in 1950 highlight this: (p.130) 'Men's ultra-smart trousers... usual pockets, extension waistband' and similarly in 1960 (p.237) 'Self-supporting trousers with extension waistband and inside brace bubuttons.' In 1970 (p.145) the word 'portly' was used: 'Consort portly fitting suit' and 'extra size range' also figured. In 1980 the clothes were advertised as 'Big Sizes Range' (1980: 465) which suggested that it is acceptable to be 'big'. The word 'big' was not used in the advertisements aimed at women. Similarly in 2000 (p.620) there was an advertisement for 'Samson Plus Pants. By Adidas.' These advertisements do not reinforce the notion of having to be thin in the way that the commercials aimed at women have done, instead being 'big' is assumed to be more acceptable for men and thus the clothing offered reflected the needs of the Catalogue's customer base.

Men: Looks

Whilst the advertisements for clothing aimed at women tended to suggest that women are to be looked at, the advertisements aimed at men tended to highlight that men are intrinsically handsome or good looking. This is a subtle difference as men already possess this characteristic whereas women need to achieve this. For example, as we commented earlier, instead of addressing men as 'you will be smart' they are assumed to be 'smart.' Thus, in 1940 (p.101) an advertisement for 'A very serviceable, good-looking suit priced exceptionally low considering its style, cut and quality,' suggests that the clothing and the man are good-looking. There is less about the man having to become good-looking. The word handsome also featured in advertisements aimed at males.[2]

2. This particular advertisement is headlined 'Style & Quality at Money-saving Prices'. Thus it 'speaks' to the consumer at a number of levels. It clearly suggests that men can wear good-looking clothing which reflects their good-looks. However, the advertisement is careful to emphasise throughout the 'value-for-money' aspect of the clothing with the repeated use of the phrase 'hard-wearing' as well as frequent mention of its price-point; in other words it is directly speaking to the aspirational working-class man who is price-conscious.

For example, 1960 (p.230) 'Men's aquatite blended woollen Tweed showerproof Coat that will give you complete pride of ownership. Beautifully cut and finished....A handsomely finished coat of value' and 'Double Jersey knitted waistcoat, handsomely cut form all wool fabric. The smart choice of every modern man.' The man is addressed as though he is already handsome whereas the advertising aimed at women tends to suggest they need to become beautiful or good looking. This is also highlighted by an advertisement in 1970 (p.414) 'Fine and dandy shirt goes colour gay and takes on the frill of a lifetime - whisk it off, the good looks remain.' Not only is this advertisement referring to the clothing that remains 'good looking' but is addressing the man as being 'good looking.' Another commercial also reinforces this (1970: 414) 'Beverly makes it long sleeved and body hugging in Pink cotton. Terrific styling with polo collar - think you look good? You're right.' This suggests that men tend to think of themselves (or are encouraged to think of themselves) as independent of any gazes, so unlike the male gaze there is no equivalent female gaze being applied to the men in these advertisements. Even if the advertisements are addressing women buying clothes for men, it is a subtle difference that is being highlighted. This is all the more remarkable given that both the agents and customers of Kays Catalogue, along with other similar catalogues, were women (Casey, 2014; Coopey et al, 2005). The advertisements in the Catalogue therefore highlight the constant hegemonic nature of the male gaze which impacts both men and women, denoting and reinforcing gender norms.

Conclusion

In Chapter One we illustrated how girls and boys become gendered through the clothes that they wear and the toys with which they play. We highlighted the ways in which the processes of co-consumption by the (usually) female primary-carer, in conjunction with the individual child, created particular forms of gendered identities, and the way in which Catalogues such as Kays were implicated in that process of consumption and identity-making. In this chapter we have identified a similar process, where the discourses used to sell adult clothing are highly gendered, even though the primary purchasers of the clothing will have been women. This is particularly significant from the 1930s onwards in relation to the use of Catalogues as women have been identified as holding 'the purse-strings in working-class families' (Coopey et al, 2005: 101). Later in the century the pattern of consumption remains the same whereby 'among couples using mail order in 1989, 67 per cent were used by the female partner alone, 30 per cent were used by both partners, but only 3 per cent were used by the male partner alone' (Coopey et al, 2005: 130-1). Thus we have here a clear example of McCracken's claim that 'catalogues are [...] very powerful meaning maker[s]. Catalogues use images and text to give meaning to products that would otherwise be quite ordinary' (2005: 189). Ugolini commenting on the lifestyles presented in advertisements and catalogues at the turn of the twentieth century suggested that they were 'desirable [lifestyles] ... rather than the lifestyles actually available to the majority of the population' (2003: 82), and Casey similarly suggests that decades later, advertisements offer spaces, particularly for working-class women, to 'day-dream, browse, choose and purchase' (2014:13).[3] We have sought to consider how far this type of consumption of the advertisements could be applied to the promotion of particular types of gender identities.

We have found that men have a much wider range of masculinities on offer through the advertising compared with the range of femininities on offer for women. The advertisements for women tend to emphasise that they should be attractive or housewives and mothers. The advertisements for men's clothing tend to emphasise work and activity: men should be sportsmen, working men and gentlemen. Additionally, the range of roles available to, and for, men change over time, as wider patterns of consumption also change (cf. Andrews, 2015; Casey, 2014; Clarke, 2007; Crane, 2000; Ugolini, 2003; Wilson, 1985). The advertisements for men offer a range of desirable masculine lifestyles, whereas for women they are centred, for most of the century, on an idealised domestic setting (cf. Andrews, 2015; Schorman, 2003; Ugolini, 2003). Moreover, we would argue that the clothing itself carries symbolic meaning, particularly in relation to the discourses around gender identities.

The gendered class identities available through the advertisements in Kays Catalogue are evident. As we have discussed above, during the course of the twentieth century class identity became less synonymous with particular styles of dress and other markers were used instead, such as 'quality' and knowing what to wear and how to wear it (cf. Entwistle, 2000: 134). This is evident in the language used to describe clothing.

It should be remembered that 'meaning [and identity] via consumption is achieved in different ways across the life-course' (Hogg and Michell, 1996: 641). The way that body images are addressed differs for men and women over the life of the Catalogue. For women, there is the notion of being slim, becoming slim or covering up if one does not achieve the desired body image. For men, there was

3. It should also be noted that the type of Catalogue itself carries symbolic meaning (Hogg and Mitchell, 1996), and this meaning will necessarily have an impact on the way in which advertisements are consumed by their readers and the possible impact this may have on the process of identity construction. Indeed the middle-class consumers of Catalogues such as Land's End and Racing Green actively disassociated themselves from traditional mail-order Catalogues (Clarke and Miller, n.d.) as they carried with them the 'stigma of restricted, credit bound consumption' (Clarke, 1998: 75).

no reference to having to be slim or thin in their advertising although this may have changed had the Catalogue survived beyond 2000. Women are presented as looking at themselves from the viewpoint of the male gaze, whereas men are presented as individuals who look at themselves from their own individual viewpoint. In conclusion we would argue that particular forms of gendered identities were therefore constructed and (re)presented across the century, in a myriad of ways through the consumption of Kays Catalogue itself and the advertisements within.

Acknowledgements
The authors would like to thank their respective families for the support given during the writing of Chapters One and Two.

References

Andrews, M. (2015) Shopping for Identities and Purchasing Fantasies of Domesticity in Post-War Kays Catalogues In B. M. Mitra & R. E. Johnson (eds.) *Gender Construction in Kays Catalogues: 1920 to the New Millennium*, Cambridge, Cambridge Academic Ltd.

Braun, V. and Clarke, V. (2006) Using thematic Analysis in Psychology. *Qualitative Research in Psychology.* Vol. (3), pp. 77-101.

Casey, E. (2014) Catalogue Communities: Work and consumption in the UK catalogue industry. *Journal of Consumer Culture.* http://joc.sagepub.com/content/early/2014/03/27/469540514528199.refs.html.

Clarke, A. (1998) Window Shopping at Home: classifieds, catalogues and new consumer skills in D. Miller (ed.) *Material Cultures: why some things matter.* Chicago: University of Chicago Press.

Clarke, A. (2007) Making Sameness: Mothering, Commerce and the Culture of Children's Birthday Parties in E. Casey & L. Martens (eds.) *Gender and Consumption*, Aldershot: Ashgate.

Clarke, A. & Miller, D. (n.d.) *Fashion and Anxiety.* Available at: http://www.ucl.ac.uk/anthropology/people/academic_staff/d_miller/mil-3 [Accessed 12.7.14]

Collinson, D. & Hearn, H. (2001) Naming Men as Men: Implications for Work, Organization and Management in S.M. Whitehead & F. J. Barrett (eds.) *The Masculinities Reader*, Cambridge: Polity.

Coopey, R. & Porter, D. (2003) Agency Mail order in Britain c. 1900-2000: Spare-time agents and their customers in J. Benson & L. Ugolini (eds.) *A Nation of Shopkeepers: Five centuries of British retailing.* London: I B Tauris & Co.

Coopey, R., O'Connell, S. & Porter, D. (2005) *Mail Order Retailing in Britain: A business and social history.* Oxford: Oxford University Press.

Crane, D. (2012) Gender and Hegemony in Fashion Magazines: Women's Interpretations of Fashion Photographs. *The Sociological Quarterly.* Vol. 4(4), pp.541-563.

Crane, D. (2000) *Fashion and its Social Agendas.* Chicago: University of Chicago Press.

Crane, D. & Bovone, L. (2006) Approaches to Material Culture: The sociology of fashion and clothing. *Poetics.* Vol. (34), pp. 319-333.

Entwistle, J. (2000) *The Fashioned Body: Fashion, dress and social theory.* Cambridge: Polity Press.

Fletcher, D.R. (2010) The Working Class? Economic Transformation, Informal Work and Male Working-Class Identity. *Social Policy and Society.* Vol. 9(3), pp. 325-336.

Green, J. D. (1967) *Birds of Britain.* New York: Macmillan.

Griffiths, C.A., Ryan, P. and Foster, J. H. (2011) Personality and Social Psychology. Thematic analysis of Antonovsky's sense of coherence theory. *Scandinavian Journal of Psychology.* Vol. 52, pp. 168-173.
Hogg, M. K. & Michell, P. C. N. (1996) Identity, Self and Consumption: a conceptual framework. *Journal of Marketing Management.* Vol. 12, pp. 629-644.
Hourigan, S.R. and Bougoure, U.-S. (2012) Towards a better understanding of fashion clothing involvement. *Australasian Marketing Journal.* Vol. 20, pp.127-135.
Jeffords, S. (1994) *Hard Bodies: Hollywood Masculinity in the Reagan Era.* New Brunswick, NJ: Rutgers University Press.
Koll-Stobbe, A. (1994) Message Merchants: Cognitive Aspects of Advertising Cultural Discourse. *Folia Linguistics.* Vol. 28(3-4), pp.385-398.
Laplanche, J. & Pontalis, J.B. (2006) *The Language of Psychoanalysis.* Reprint, London: Karnac Books Ltd.
Lazaroiu, G. (2012) Communicative functions of smart clothing. *Contemporary Readings in Law and Social Justice.* Vol. 4(1), pp.162-167.
MacKinnon, K. (2003) *Representing Men, Maleness and Masculinity in the Media.* London: Arnold.
Martin, M. and Muthukrishna, N. (2011) Deconstructed discourses of gender equality in cross-gender friendships: grade seven boys and girls in an inner-city school. *Gender & Behaviour.* Vol. 9(1), pp. 3798-3811.
Matheson, D. (2005) *Media Discourses. Analysing Media Texts.* Maidenhead: Open University Press, McGraw Hill Education.
Mayne, I. (2000) The Inescapable Images: Gender and Advertising. *Equal Opportunities International.* Vol. 19(2-4), pp.56-61.
McCracken, G. (2005) *Culture and Consumption II: Markets, meanings and brand management.* Bloomington, IN: Indiana Press.
Miller, D. (1991) *Material Culture and Mass Consumption.* Cambridge, Massachusetts: Blackwell.
Mulvey, L. (1989) *Visual and Other Pleasures.* Basingstoke: Macmillan.
Redmond, S. (2003) Thin White Women in Advertising. *Journal of Consumer Culture.* Vol. 3(2), pp. 170-190.
Ross, J.A. and Green, C. (2011) Inside the experience of Anorexia Nervosa: A thematic analysis. *Counselling and Psychotherapy Research.* June Vol. 11(2), pp.112-119.
Schorman, R. (2003) *Selling Style: Clothing and social change at the turn of the century.* Philadelphia: University of Pennsylvania Press.

// Chapter 3 //
Shopping for Identities and Purchasing Fantasies of Domesticity in post-war Kays Catalogues

Maggie Andrews

Historians such as Rappaport and Lancaster have long paid attention to the growth of department and chain stores in charting the rise of consumer culture in the late nineteenth and twentieth century. This chapter draws upon an examination of 1950s and early 1960s Kays Catalogues to demonstrate how such catalogues offer scope to research domestic purchasing of not merely products such as saucepans, china, rugs and sheets but also of domestic identities, fantasies and aspirations for housewives during this period when wartime rationing came to an end and the post-war consumer boom began. It draws upon some of the analytical frameworks of recent anthropological work on shopping consumer culture, most notably that of McCracken (1988), Miller (1998) and Bourdieu (2010) and historical work on consumer culture, domesticity, homes and housing by, for example Langhamer (2005), and Giles (2004). A key element of much of this work is the importance of the domestic as both a lived experience and as a site of the imagination whilst the consumer is discussed not as a passive dupe of advertising or capitalist industries but as an active and discerning agent making meaning through purchases and the acquisition of material artefacts. First it is perhaps important to say a word or two about my use of the term *fantasy,* for in using it I intend to draw attention to the significance for many people not merely of their everyday and mundane material environment but also of the world of the imagination. Thus for a historian looking at Kays Catalogues, fantasies, fears and aspirations are important as they shed light on what Raymond Williams has described as 'the structure of feeling'(1980) of a particular historical era. Furthermore, it will be argued, they offered to the ordinary housewife one way of negotiating the gap between lived experience and their fantasies.

The domestic space, a place called home was disrupted by the Second World War in ways not seen before or since in British industrialised society. The everyday practices and routines of families were fractured by the conscription of men, and from 1941, of women into the armed forces and war-work, evacuation, billeting and the new patterns of both paid and voluntary work. At the same time, the home, the family occupying a domestic space, the aspiration of so many in the inter-war years, was elevated as an ideal to be fought for and protected. Civilians were encouraged to 'keep the home fires burning' although for many their domestic life was increasingly unstable and the idealisation of home and family became intrinsically entwined with everyday fantasies of the post-war peace. Thus, as Giles points out domesticity, the home, was and remained, 'an arena in which women experience and live out.... fantasies' (2004: 3).

In the contemporary era the lexicon of images which feed such fantasies are varied and include lifestyle television and a bit of house-porn on Rightmove, but both these had their predecessors, areas which the historian can explore to glean the fantasies and imagination of women in any particular era and women's magazines, radio, film, advertising. Debra Ryan's work has shown how the Ideal Home Exhibition, for example, 'pandered to women's rational needs and consumerist fantasies' promoting acceptable envy. Like the Ideal Home Exhibition, Kays Catalogues provide 'insights into the neglected history of hopes, dreams and aspirations' (2000: 17) of domesticity, albeit those of particular social groups. Indeed the Kays reader can be described as suburban or rural lower middle-class or respectable working class, provincial rather than trend-setting.

As Langhamer's analysis of Mass Observation has noted, many young women during the war were preoccupied with thoughts of marriage (2003) and Pat Thane has pointed out 'after the Second World War marriage, at least once, became almost universal' (2005: 47) and within marriage it was assumed women would take on the domestic responsibilities of a housewife, managing relationships, consumption, budgets and household chores. Fulfilling these responsibilities in practice was however for many unexpectedly challenging, little wonder perhaps then that for women fantasies of home became so important. A third of a million servicemen, servicewomen and merchant seaman had been killed as well as approximately 70,000 civilians during the war and two and half million couples had been apart for long periods of time (P. Addison and H. Jones 2005). Fragile and tentative family units struggled in the post-war era; snippets of their struggle can be glimpsed in the problem pages of *Women's Weekly* magazine and letters to the BBC's *Woman's Hour* as they struggled with financial hardship, rationing and personal relationships. Their difficulties were exaggerated by the problem of finding a suitable space to turn into a place called home. Despite the speculative building of the inter-war period, which had provided new suburban houses for many of the middle classes, the legacy of wartime bombing was a severe shortage of housing stock and a significant number of damaged houses: nearly one million in London alone. The 1945-51 the Labour Government in allocating limited resources and skilled workers prioritised repairs (N. Bullock,

2005). Nevertheless in 1949, as *Picture Post* pointed out, a survey suggested that the Labour Government's second most outstanding failure was seen as being 'too slow with housing' (2005: 344).

The post-war housing shortage forced one in five households in 1951 to share a home, either with strangers or as 'concealed households' living with in-laws. In 1950 approximately one in six London households' inhabitants lived in buildings converted for multiple occupancy, often each household in a single room sharing a sink, tap and lavatory, with an allocated day for washing. The gap between the lived experience of domesticity and what Langhamer has identified as the fantasy of home, offering warmth, cosiness and the ability to be oneself so central to post-war aspiration (2005: 345), led to justifiable dissatisfaction. Thus in the 1950s, for many, the idealised domesticity and family, so longed for during the war, did not live up to expectations; Kays Catalogues however offered a range of stepping stones towards the still cherished ideal of home. McCracken has suggested that consumer items are often a way of attempting to reconcile the gap between people's idealised lives and their lived experience; consumer purchases can be seen as stepping stones or scaffolding towards these ideals (1998). The purchase of items from the Kays Catalogue, large or small according to budgets, was the first step along the way to the longed-for home life that proved so elusive. The presentation of ranges of items: cookware, china, bedding and soft-furnishings, which could be purchased individually but which together will transform the home, enabled each individual item, even if only a butter dish or a new tea towel, to be a small step towards the longed for and indeed fought for domestic ideal. The linguistic phrasing used within Kays Catalogues to describe consumer objects suggested that they were signifiers of modernity and also a cosy 'being oneself' domesticity; terms such as 'comfort, warmth, quality', were intertwined with 'modern, beauty, efficiency, convenience, streamlined and colourful' in descriptions of items of kitchenware, bedding and soft furnishings in the 1950s. Each term operates as a signifier of a fantasy of domesticity and suggests to housewives that what they were lacking in their old, ugly, inefficient, inconvenient, cheap, and dull homes was a consumer goodie. In catalogue purchases lay the promise of ideal domesticity.

Britain's financial crisis at the end of the Second World War, with large debts to the USA, meant that a period of austerity had quickly followed the victory celebrations; not only did rationing remain but it got more severe with, for example, bread being rationed for the first time in 1946. The austerity was metaphorically emphasised by the hard winter of 1947 which provoked a fuel crisis. As Addison suggests, in the late 1940s 'the Home Front ran on without a war to sustain it' (1985: 34) and with a legacy of pent up consumer demand from wartime, the era of austerity was also accompanied by despondency, weariness and a flourishing black-market operated by spivs. Acknowledging the spirit of the time, in the 1950s the Kays Catalogues carry references to items for the home which will 'save time and labour'. In the drab days of the early 1950s brightness was eulogised, 'Have a brighter home now and pay later' it was suggested to customers who were encouraged to purchase mirrors, brass candlesticks, a brass candelabra or a retractable hearth brush in 1952, (1952: 178) or were guided towards 'Your opportunity to brighten your kitchen' (1952: 215) But stylistically these were very different versions of brightening up a home, brass candlesticks offered a traditional cosiness, plastic kitchen utensils a new youthful modernity.

The idea of shopping as a widespread leisure activity for women, which historians such as Rappaport suggest developed in London department stores, alongside exhibitions, in the early part of the twentieth century and which became an activity of entertainment and pleasure (1996), was undermined by the Second World War. The introduction of rationing and queues in the 1940s, arguably turned shopping into a chore rather than entertainment. Alternatively catalogue shopping offered what Alison Clarke has described as 'window shopping at home' (1997) with, importantly in the early 1950s, an absence of queues and an abundance of purchasable items enabling shopping, like women's magazines, to operate as something of a 'mental chocolate box' (Winship, 1987) Thus in Winter 1954 the Kays Catalogue emphasised the benefits of 'Armchair shopping' whereby:

> in the comfort of your own home you may leaf through this catalogue with time to study the illustrations and facts about things you want to buy. In no other way can you have the comfort and convenience which is yours when shopping by post from the catalogue (1954: 82).

The work of shopping, the time-consuming trudging of so much 1940s and early 1950s consumption was able to be replaced by perusing the catalogue in the reassuringly familiar domestic space which allowed shopping to once again become a pleasurable leisure activity, just as surfing the net, putting things in online baskets or on wish lists is now. In doing so, Kays put the catalogue experience on a par with reading a magazine, something to be indulged in over a tea break. The relaxed nature of catalogue shopping is emphasised by the idea of the friendly Kays representative who interestingly is pictured in the catalogue as a middle aged male, trustworthy, a little paternalistic and reassuring, although records indicate that this role was more often undertaken by a woman who was a friend or at least a familiar neighbour of the shopper.

Arguably catalogue shopping does more than save the drudgery of trailing around shops and re-introducing entertainment into purchases, for as McCracken points out the place and channel of marketing contributes to the meanings of consumer goods (2005). Viewed in the home, catalogues are domesticated, they carry with them the reassuring associations of idealised domesticity; they are comforting, familiar. The domestic associations of the catalogue, the reliable, traditional associations of the Kays Company, established in the nineteenth century and based in Worcester, with iconic images of the Cathedral city on the catalogue cover, enabled it to establish a reassuring brand identity of comfortable, reliable, dependable Britishness. This enabled Kays to take up a discursive tone which appeared to offer guidance to its domestic purchasers although the tone could also perhaps be interpreted as offering governance (see Winship, 2000).

For the potential customers who leafed through the pages of Kays Catalogues, very much more frequently than they purchased anything, the catalogues also offered pleasurable fantasies based upon 'what if'. What if I purchase this new record player ... brides delight sheets, etc. Each item was potentially the first rung on the ladder or a stepping stone towards one of a range of idealised domesticities, each offered one of multiple alternative, but overlapping, identities implied by these domesticities. Housewives could position themselves in one of a range of identity positions and lifestyle choices as they leafed their way through the catalogue. Three popular housewifely identities established in the inter-war period which can be glimpsed re-appearing in the post-war world are: the skilled cook and domestic guru, the modern housewife who adhered to the principles of scientific management and finally the all-important good manager and rational consumer.

The 1950s skilled cook and domestic guru became an increasingly appealing identity position, on offer to those perusing Kays Catalogues, particularly as rationing eased in the late 1950s alongside an increase in leisure, the introduction of foreign travel and a growing emphasis upon culinary enjoyment. Kays was however more mundane and down to earth than the fanciful writings of the increasingly popular gastronome of the period, Elizabeth David, who introduced 'moods of relaxed pleasure' and suggested 'the search for food and description of it is a very serious matter in intellectual, cultural and artistic terms' (Floyd 2003). A broadening range of products were certainly available in supermarkets (Benson: 69) but access to such foods and even to supermarkets was not by any means uniformly available to a woman. For the suburban, rural and middle-England shoppers from Kays the exotic food, including aubergines, portrayed in films such as *Genevieve* (1953) were apparitional only. Kays offered instead a 'new 22 piece household helpers pack' or a 'wonder kitchen set,' complete with Swiss roll tins

(1952: 300) which suggested consumers could 'smile your chores away'. The use of the term 'chore' suggests that cake-baking and domestic skills were for many not yet a leisure activity although they remained core housewifely skills.

Alternatively the efficient housewife utilising scientific management and modern methods to rationalise her housework was suggested by various labour saving devices which apparently made household chores light work and included automatic duchess and rotary potato peelers. Under the heading 'Housewives choice for saving labour' promoting pressure cookers and vacuum cleaners, consumers were encouragingly assured that the purchase of a particular vacuum cleaner would, due to 'the ease with which your cleaning can be carried out with the GEC cleaner... give many more hours for leisure relaxed in the knowledge your home is kept spotlessly clean' (1950: 215). Arguably the consumer was not so easily persuaded that any hoover would turn 1950s housewifely drudgery into a lifestyle with ample leisure but rather the catalogue plays with the possibility of being the sort of ideal housewife who has things under control, and has scope for a leisurely cup of tea with a friend rather than running constantly from pillar to post.

Within working class culture of the mid-twentieth century; the 'burden of domestic survival fell' (Tebbutt, 1995: 11) upon the housewife who was 'discursively constructed as a manager of home and all importantly the budget' (Roberts, 1984: 125). Skills in domestic management in many respects defined working class housewives; Kays payment methods, in regular instalments, could be seen to re-enforce this domestic identity of the housewife as a good manager, whilst accompanying thriftiness was encouraged in a range of offers which suggested that the housewife was making savings by careful choice of purchases, for example by gaining the better price offered when making a multi-purchases of tea towels. The Kays Catalogue frequently addressed its reader as the rational consumer, who by carefully studying the range of goods and clearly marked prices in the catalogue was able to identify the best buys. Her skill in buying more economical but better quality items, thereby maximising her family's welfare by her good household management, was reinforced when it was explained: 'there is a satisfaction in owning the finest... and experience teaches that you save most in the long run when you buy the BEST quality' (1955: 45). It was the easily available credit provided by Kays, in an era before the common use of credit cards and when overdrafts were hard to come by, which coaxed the housewife into having the pleasure of purchase and acquisition buttressed by the reassurance that she was managing her family's expenditure wisely. Thus the products and the credit terms, which offered a phased and predictable expenditure apparently allowed 'Thousands of British People' to manage their household 'money worries' (1957: 33).

Furthermore as rationing was replaced by the new consumer boom, Kays Catalogues suggested that for many the way forward to their consumerist aspirations lay in credit which could provide the first step up towards their domestic ideal:

> 'This is the kitchen I've always dreamed of .... but I never thought I should get it so soon' says Jean . Most of the cooking utensils and furniture were from Kays. Again Jean and her husband used Kays continuous credit to increase their buying power when planning the sort of Kitchen Jean had always wanted (1957: 88).

For the few who might conceivably buy their kitchen on credit through Kays many thousands more, who lived in less salubrious accommodation, could buy a little part of that dream by purchasing kitchen utensils, pans or even a drop door food safe. (The latter being a plastic container which kept food safe from the rodents who also strove to make their homes in much of the rather poor, un-modernised post-war housing available.)

An important facet in the discourses which encouraged the use of credit was the notion of realising the aspirational dream of an ideal modern kitchen, 'lovely bedroom' etc. which would bring the admiration, even envy of friends and neighbours. Credit could enable householders to live, as the saying goes, beyond their means, and headings on pages explaining credit terms which read 'We were so much better off than we thought' are interestingly acknowledging fantasies of social aspiration. Credit would enable people, it was suggested, to gain the distinctive accoutrements of being a little higher up the social scale, in an era where social scientists were soon to talk of embourgiosement and the Conservative Prime Minster allegedly asserted that ' the class war is over and we have won it'.

As the acquisition of objects often may serve to carry narratives of lives and associations that had been restrained by rationing for over 14 years, perhaps it is not surprising that Kays Catalogues offered pages of china. Purchasing china is incompatible with the fragility of homes under threat from bombing and thus in the 1950s suggests an affirmation of the post-war domestic world as solid, physically secure. In the wide range of china and pottery offered to the 1959 housewives who perused the pages of Kays Catalogues there was a choice not merely of artefacts but of stylistic statements of identity. The Catalogue choices of china facilitated women placing themselves within a range of substrata of class, age and lifestyles distinctions. Gold stamp, fine bone china suggested an aristocratic, some might say, a pretentious style; alternatively Harlequin

Staffordshire Earthenware had a colourful contemporary gaiety, whilst the tea set decorated with Devonshire thatched cottages apparently brought 'beauty and the picturesque' to purchasers meal times (Spring/ Summer 1959: 42).

Housing remained a political priority and as the economy adjusted onto a peacetime footing the Conservative government stimulated house building with the 1952 Macmillan Housing Act and by 1957 two and a half million houses had been built since the war fuelling the 1950s interest in home making (L. Hoskins 2004: 4) which was given an extra boost by the end of rationing in 1954 and the introduction of commercial television in 1955. Thus by 1956 the pages of the Kays Catalogues heralded a new era of consumer culture, with colour and variety virtually springing off the pages of the catalogues as the commentary emphasised the importance of treats and indulgence as well as thrift.

The privatized home life that new improved housing offered was the dream of many middle and working class people. It was achievable through hard work, as well as consumer culture, or perhaps more accurately by hard work and consumer culture as DIY entered the English language in 1958, and a plethora of men's tools appeared in the Kay Catalogues expanding the potential for home improvement beyond the ability to create: 'New Rooms for old with Kays modern wallpapers' which apparently made 'decorating a pleasure' (1952: 163) in the 1950s. A range of modernising home improvement activities suggested, for example, covering surfaces in older houses with hygienic and brightly coloured Formica which was, for many, a symbol of modernity (J. Brown 2000). Kays Catalogues suggested a range of ways to bring such modernity into housewives' kitchens; each one a rung on the ladder towards the ideal fantasy kitchen which featured 'free standing kitchen units' – which were 'labour saving, durable Formica topped and easy to clean' (1957: 402). 'The streamlined modern Kitchen' that was apparently 'A joy to work in' encapsulated both the colourfulness and the modernity of the new post-rationing era. It could be attained by purchasing a range of kitchen units or step by step, through small purchases of individual colourful furniture, china and kitchenware which was 'designed to blend with' home purchasers 'favourite colour scheme' (1957: 402) each item promised the attainability of the ideal domestic home, signified by an ideal kitchen.

Whilst acknowledging the significance of the kitchen and cooking to 1950s constructions of housewifery, there is an element of trying a little too much, perhaps in many of these features in the Kays Catalogues, an element of 'performativity' (J. Butler 2006) or perhaps desperation in them. For example the reference to 'cheerfulness' in the two page spread in 1957 on Jury Glass on Steel Jetware suggested:

> Life in the kitchen takes on a new cheerfulness when you cook with Jury Jetware. The saucepans have a gleaming porcelain enamel body, a special vapour-seal lid, a heat resisting handle in plastic with a disc and knob – also in plastic – to protect the fingers against contact with hot surfaces. In the charm of brilliant contemporary house and garden colours there is no equal in Jetware (1957: 262-263).

They were indeed gleaming – gleaming yellow, and in plastic which operated as a signifier of modernity, hygiene and the new Elizabethan age, as it was referred to at the time. Colour was by no means restricted to the kitchen as one woman recalled:

> I've got the sideboard and the studio couch. They were very fashionable in the 1950s….It was black with little bits of red and yellow on it that went well with cherry red armchair and the mid-brown furniture and the rug in front of the fire that had a red, yellow and white zigzag pattern (quoted in A. Hecht, 2001: 16).

An enthusiasm for consumer artefacts is hardly surprising in a nation that had either lost or seen the destruction of many of their possessions in wartime due to the effects of bombing, dislocation, looting and crime. Nevertheless, although by 1959 Conservative politician Harold Macmillan confidently asserted 'most of our people had never had it so good', the consumer boom was not enjoyed by all; a persistent strand of poverty remained. Housing remained a political issue well into the sixties articulated in the television play *Cathy Come Home* (BBC 1966). Arguably, the housing crisis can also be seen as a direct consequence of increased expectations that went hand-in-hand with consumerism, the welfare state and the post-war settlement which Sinfield suggests was premised on a continued improvement in living standards (1997). The desire to participate in domestic consumer culture led an increasing number of couples to seek to set up their own households at a young age. This situation, alongside many older people remaining in their homes at an older age put pressure on the housing stock. The population of England had grown from 38 million in 1921 to 46 million in 1960s and the number of private households almost doubled from 8.7 to 14.9 million (Macfarlan, 1981).

Consequently as Arthur Marwick has pointed out the 'majority of the population continued to live in late nineteenth and early twentieth century homes badly in need of updating' which provided 'squalid and overcrowded housing' (1996: 87), thus the Ministry of Housing and Local Authorities classed approximately

1,800,000 houses as unfit for human habitation in 1967 (Macfarlan 1981: 63). Many rural homes remained without any piped water and Kays Catalogue catered for such customers; they could order chemical loos in 1959, and rolls of a thick plastic wall liner for kitchens which could be used to cover a multitude of housing sins and give the illusion of hygienic modernity featured regularly in the 1950s and 1960s. Even those on limited incomes in poor housing were thus offered stepping stones, rungs on the ladder, towards their fantasy of an ideal domestic space. Such stepping stones might be mundane: brightly coloured butter dishes, plastic table clothes and potato peelers but they were linked within the physical boundaries of the Kays Catalogue to images of more idealised domestic settings. These purchases were made easier, attainable by credit as the catalogue explained: 'When you buy on easy payments you can buy EXTRA things.. a new blouse to go with your new costume....nice things for your home... books and games for the children (1952: 278). By purchasing a small item customers were able to identify with the 'world of Kays' for as McCracken suggests: 'Great catalogues make meaning so powerfully that it is not unusual to hear consumers say they 'want to live in the catalogue' (2005: 189).

Living in the Catalogue was not merely a consumerist fantasy of products and purchases, rather these products become props in fantasies of idealised family relationships. Domestic homes are not merely physical space but are invested with meanings through lived relationships, although in the post-war era home, the domestic space was perceived to be a place of mundane belonging and as Giles suggests, seen as a 'refuge from the repressions and alienations of modernity'...... a place , '.... in which the injuries of modern living can be healed' (2004: 9), for many housewives the lived experience of home in post-war Britain was less than ideal. Divorce reformers pointed to the empty shell many marriages had become in the era and popular culture seethed with the potentially disruptive behaviour beneath the veneer of respectability in films such as *It Always Rains on Sunday* (1947), *Mandy* (1952) and *Woman in a Dressing Gown* (1957) for example. Material culture and consumer purchases played a role in forming, maintaining, negotiating and attempting to construct the domestic family. Looked at in this way the rolls of plastic covering for kitchen walls, were not just an attempt to cover up the physical inadequacies of the post-war kitchens but also attempts to cover up the fractured families which were proving hard to put back together after the disruption and separation of wartime. As McCracken points out, creating the ideal home is about shaping the ideal family that fits in it; homes are 'transformational opportunities' (2005: 21). Crafting the home, through do-it-yourself, purchasing and domestic labour was about crafting the family that was to live there. If as Miller suggests shopping 'is primarily an act of love that in its daily conscientiousness becomes one of the means by which relationships of love and care are constituted by practice' (1998: 18), it is little wonder that, in the late 1950s, housewives were susceptible to Kays catalogues' encouragement to buy not only 'books and games for the children' (1957: 302) but many other items for their families. For customers in the post-war period rising consumer culture, the catalogues easy-payment instalments offered the possibility of realising their idealised fantasy of home.

In buying objects for a family member or partner, housewives, Miller suggests are involved in a process of constructing the recipient of such a purchase or gift as the sort of person, the sort of family, who appreciates the purchases. It is within such an approach to purchasing that the frequent use of the term 'quality' used to describe items in the Kays catalogues can be best understood. Items described as having 'quality' appealed to the housewife because the 'quality' referred not just to catalogue items but to the housewife's family for whom she made her purchases. Many housewives saw their 'role as selecting goods which are intended to be educative, uplifting and in a rather vague sense morally superior' (Miller, 1998: 18). Although quite what the recipients of the chromium plated bird cage, an auto controlled electric iron and Pifco Electric massager included in the 1950 catalogue under the heading 'To please the family' were being constructed into, remains a bit of a mystery. (However, apparently the massager was 'an aid to beauty and to relieve pain. Designed on advanced scientific principles' whereby 'in the privacy of your own home and at your convenience you can carry out expensive treatments practised by masseurs and in beauty parlours' .... reassuringly a full instructional leaflet was enclosed (1952: 272-3). If the rhetoric around these last items seems a little bizarre, then I would suggest that this is consistent with the post-war era in which there are indications of housewives trying just a little too hard to create the post- war domestic world that the war had been fought for and for which they longed. The Kays Catalogues offered snippets to housewives of what appears to be purchasable and hence attainable signifiers of their fantasies of ideal domesticity. Kitchens utensils suggested a range of housewifely identities, china class or lifestyle position. Gifts for family offered the possibility that loved ones could be moulded into the housewives ideal. If there is something a little over the top about increasing excessive, unstable even, performative domestic femininity perhaps this is not surprising. Rather it can be seen as a signal of the forthcoming cultural revolution of the sixties and early seventies (see Marwick, 1998) when for some at least there is a scope to engage in a very different approach to the gap between lived experience and fantasies of domesticity. For others of course the Kays Catalogues continued to offer purchases which promised to be stepping stones towards ideal domesticity.

References

Addison, P. (1985) *The Road to 1945*, London: Pimlico.
Addison P. and Jones H. (eds). (2005) *A Companion to Contemporary Britain 1939–2000*, Oxford: Blackwell Publishing.
Benson, J. (1994) *The Rise of Consumer Society in Britain 1880-1990*, London: Longman.
Bourdieu, P. (2010) *Distinction; A Social Critique of the Judgement of Taste*, Oxford: Routlege.
Bullock, N. (2005) 'Re-assessing the Post-War housing Achievement: the impact of War –Damage Repairs on the New Housing Programme in London' in *Twentieth Century British History* Vol 16 no 3, pp256-282.
Butler, J. (2006) *Gender Trouble*: Feminism and the Subversion of Identity, Oxford: Routlege.
Brown, J. (2000) 'Decisions in DIY : women, home improvements and advertising in post-war Britain' in Andrews, M. and Talbot, M. *All the World and Her Husband*, London: Cassell.
Clarke, A. (1997) 'Window Shopping at home, class, catalogues and new consumer skills' in Miller, D (ed*) Material Cultures: Why Some things Matter*, Oxford: Routledge.
Floyd, J. (2003) 'Simple Honest Food: Elizabeth David and the Construction of Nation in Cookery Writing' in Floyd, J. and Forster, L. (2003 and 2010) *The Recipe Reader*, University of Nebraska Press.
Giles, J. (2004) *The Parlour and the Suburb: Domestic Identities, Class, Femininity and Modernity*, London: Berg.
Hecht, A. (2001) 'Home Sweet Home' in Miller D. *Home Possessions*, London: Berg.
Hoskins, L. (2004) *Fiftiestyle*, London: Middlesex University Press (for the Museum of Domestic Design and Architecture).
Kays Catalogues 1950-1960, *World of Kays*. University of Worcester Research Collections. Available at http://www.worldofkays/org/
Lancaster, Bill. (2000) *The Department Store a Social History*, Leicester University Press.
Langhamer, C. (2003) 'A Public House is for all classes, men and women alike': women , leisure and drink in Second World War England' in *Women's History Review*, 12:3 423-443.
Langhamer, C. (2005) 'The Meaning of Home in Post-War Britain' in *Journal of Contemporary History*, 2005 vol 40 pp 341-362.
Macfarlan, L.J. (1981) *Issues in British Politics*, Harlow: Longman.
McCracken, G. (1988) *Culture and Consumption: New Approaches to the Symbolic Character of Consumer Goods and Activities*, Minneapolis, Indiana

UniversityPress.
McCracken, G. (2005) *Culture and Consumption II: Markets, meaning and Brand Management*, Indiana: Indiana University Press.
Marwick, A. (1996), *British Society Since 1945.* London: Penguin.
Marwick, A. (1998) *The Sixties Cultural Revolution in Britain, France, Italy and the United States,*Oxford: Oxford University Press.
Miller, D. (1998) *A Theory of Shopping,* Cambridge: Polity Press.
Rappaport, E. (1996) 'The Halls of Temptation: Gender, Politics and the Construction of the Department Stores in Victorian London' in *The Journal of British Studies* Vol 35.01 pp 58-83.
Roberts, E. (1984) *A Woman's Place: An Oral History of Working Class Women 1890-1940,* Oxford: Blackwell.
Ryan, D. (2000) 'All the World and her Husband' in Andrews, M. and Talbot, M. (ed.) *All the World and Her Husband*, London: Cassell. pp 10-22.
Sinfield, A. (1997) *Literature, Politics and Culture in Postwar Britain,* London: Continuum.
Tebbutt, M. (1995) *Women's Talk? A Social History of 'Gossip' in Working Class Neighbourhoods, 1880-1960,* Aldershot: Scholar Press.
Thane, P. (2005) 'Population and the Family' in 2005 Addison P. and Jones H. (eds). (2005) *A Companion to Contemporary Britain 1939–2000*, Oxford: Blackwell Publishing.
Williams, R. (1980) *Culture and Materialism*, London: Verso.
Winship, J. (1987) *Inside Women's Magazines*, London: Pandora Press.
Winship, J. (2000) 'New Disciplines for Women and the rise of the chain store in the 1930s' in Andrews, M. and Talbot, M. (eds.) *All the World and Her Husband*, London: Cassell.

// Chapter 4 //
Worlds within *Kays*: British Modernity and Representations of Place in the 1960s

Rachel Ritchie

In September 1969, *Woman* magazine featured an advertisement for Kays home shopping Catalogue. The advertisement's one image shows a seemingly timeless illustration of Worcester Cathedral, surrounded by some other old buildings, with fields and the River Severn in the foreground (*Woman* September 27 1969: 71). This almost ahistoric picture was used on the front of the Autumn/Winter 1969 Catalogue and the emphasis on Worcester, the home of Kay & Co, was reiterated in the cover's 'Kays of Worcester' tagline. The image indicates the important position of the city in the company's corporate image. As this study demonstrates, Worcester had meaning, representing values important to the firm's brand identity. Moreover, Worcester was not the only location imbued with significance. If we look within the catalogues, we find a whole world of different places, with various connotations associated with each one. This chapter explores this 'geographical imagination' (Matless 2012: 13), drawing on an understanding of 'place' as 'not just a physical terrain but a social environment of shared meanings' (Strub 2008: 386). It investigates the symbolic geography and ascribed meanings, not reality; as Marianne Lien argues, a product can undergo a 'thorough and radical process of recontexualisation' whereby its origins become 'less important than the particular purpose it may serve' for the consumer (2000: 168).

This chapter begins by examining the role of the region compared to depictions of the metropolis. It then moves onto representations of holidaying abroad, considering links between these images and portrayals of the provincial and the capital. Whilst being a case study of Kays catalogue, the investigation also contributes to a number of important debates about post-war Britain. Firstly, it is part of a growing body of literature presenting more nuanced histories of the 1960s. For example, Frank Mort's work on London shows how social geography and understandings of the past influenced contemporary discourses and constructions of post-war modernity (2006; 2007). By demonstrating that socio-cultural change did not follow a straightforward progressive narrative, such accounts challenge ongoing myths about the decade that often rely on unfavourable comparisons with the 1950s and misrepresent minority counter-culture as mainstream (Thomas 2002; Wilson 1980). Arthur Marwick, for instance, described the 1960s as a reaction to the 1950s, claiming the later decade witnessed a cultural revolution (1998).

The desire to question this standpoint is fundamental to the way that I approached the catalogues. To establish a discrete overview of the decade as a whole, I analysed the twenty covers that appeared between 1960 and 1969. I then selected the rest of the sample based around *Time* magazine's April 1966 declaration that London was 'The Swinging City', as this soubriquet (and the broader moniker of the 'Swinging Sixties') encapsulates the Cultural Revolution view of the decade. *Time* magazine's declaration also represents a rare example of a concrete 'moment' being identified in relation to a nebulous cultural concept. In order to both critically engage with the notion of a cultural revolution and be involved in 'constructing a more complex narrative of contemporary sexual and moral change' (Mort 2006: 132), I looked at one catalogue from before this date (Spring/Summer 1965) and one from after (S/S 1968). The lapse of two years allows for production times. Within these catalogues, the focus is on visual representations of place in womenswear and menswear.

Work on post-war British modernity provides a crucial backdrop to this revisionist stance on the 1960s. The seminal *Moments of Modernity* edited collection sets out 'to interrogate the dominant narratives of post-war history' (Conekin et al 1999: 4), highlighting the contradictory impulses of British modernity, its hybrid nature and its often Janus-face, looking backwards to the past and forwards to the future. For example, there were tensions within understandings of national identity and 'Britishness' throughout the post-1945 period. On the one hand, there were hopes of the 1953 Coronation ushering in a 'second Elizabethan age' (Conekin et al 1999: 1). On the other, contemporary concerns about 'the fragility of national feeling' led to reassessments of national identity and international outlook (Conekin 2003: 17). As Chris Waters argues, 'Britain's failure to generate new narratives of national purpose ... led to a veritable crisis of national self-representation in the 1950s'; similarly, in the 1960s, 'new racism' emerged as Britishness was also becoming a fashionable phenomenon (Waters 1997: 208, 236-7). Such arguments resonate here. Modernity is a key concept throughout, with the chapter illustrating its centrality in representations of different places while accentuating its multi-faceted nature. In addition, the chapter demonstrates the inextricable links between visions of modernity and understandings of national identity. In doing so, overlaps with and points of departure from existing accounts of mid-twentieth century British modernity become apparent, particularly as themes prevalent in literature on the post-war period are also central in this account, notably race, sexuality, social class and gender.

With regards to the latter, work on modernity is again important. Explorations of gender and modernity frequently destabilise standard definitions of modernity by emphasising the alternative versions of modernity apparent in women's experiences. In relation to inter-war years, Judy Giles argues that the complex 'expressions of modernity' developed through suburban homes and domesticity are incompatible with conventional frameworks of modernity that take masculine experience as the norm; the city and the suburb 'express two different ways of responding to modernisation' (Giles 2004: 11, 35). By drawing attention to the alternative versions of modernity in circulation, such writings have helped to undermine grand narratives about 'progress' and socio-cultural transformation across the middle decades of the twentieth century. Like recent work on the 1960s, they demonstrate that change was often gradual and does not neatly fit into chronological boundaries. Furthermore, these accounts reveal that shifts did not always happen in the ways that conform to established paradigms. As historians, we must be alert to the alternative visions that the evidence may present to us – an important notion in this investigation.

Another area to which this chapter contributes is the diverse range of studies concerned with the role of place and location. Various scholars, including Mort, have shown that focusing on a particular place can yield rewards in terms of understandings of British modernity. Contributors looking at the British documentary film movement in a 2012 issue of *Twentieth Century British History*, for instance, explore the 'multiplicity of British spatial identities' (Anthony and Mansell 2012: 6). Similarly, this study explores the overlap and layering of identities and meanings within Kays, emphasising the intertwining of regional, national and international. That Worcester is a provincial city with no obvious links to fashionable 1960s scenes is critical to this endeavour, providing an ideal opportunity to probe the heavily metropolitan perspective at the heart of the cultural revolution image of the decade. As Elizabeth Wilson notes, '"swinging London" might always be a far cry from Wigan or Ipswich' (Wilson 1980: 7). One could easily substitute Wigan for Worcester.

The region and the metropolis: representations of Worcester(shire) and London

The Autumn/Winter 1969 cover image, reproduced in the *Woman* advertisement, indicated Worcester's important position in Kay & Co's identity. This becomes even more apparent when all twenty 1960s covers are considered. Whereas only one showed a generic rural scene (S/S 1967), sixteen (80%) featured Worcester or the surrounding area. The majority were photographs of prominent and easily identifiable local landmarks. Shots showing both Worcester Cathedral and the

(Kays Catalogue, 1963:1, Autumn and Winter)

neighbouring River Severn were most common (for examples, see S/S 1961; Autumn/Winter 1961; S/S 1963; S/S 1965), although the cathedral's neighbouring Edgar Tower and the Malvern hills appeared too (S/S 1962; S/S 1969). One went slightly further afield, showing Broadway in the Cotswolds (a/w 1962). In some ways, this emphasis on the company's location is unsurprising. Kay & Co were a long established Worcester firm and a major local employer. Worcester provided a useful motif in establishing a brand identity and differentiating Kays from other mail order firms. Covers have a vital role in this, as they are crucial in attracting interest and reader identification. As provincial shoppers were a major market for all kinds of home shopping catalogues, such as *Habitat* (Heathcote, 2004), Kay & Co may have seen their regional location as a way of appealing to this demographic.

The specific imagery used in representations of Worcester(shire) further suggests that the company's location functioned as a useful marketing tool. There is an aura of timelessness to many of the covers, especially those featuring the cathedral. This creates a sense of longevity and implies through association that Kay & Co is an age-old firm that is trustworthy and dependable. The cover commemorating the city's English Civil War battle reinforces this, as do covers stating 'Established in the reign of George III' (S/S 1960; a/w 1960; a/w 1964). Such evocations of 'presumed common past' drew on a vision of 'an all white, self-contained British nation', a 'united white "we"' (Conekin 2003: 193, 196) and do not acknowledge the huge rise in immigration from places such as the West Indies, India and Pakistan in the 1950s and 60s. However, this imagery is also suggestive of contemporary concerns about race; as Bill Schwarz notes, 'that "the fact of whiteness" had to be asserted at such volume, and so insistently, indicated the depth of the transformations underway' (Schwarz 1999: 191). Indeed, this discourse echoes across all the covers showing the region: 'through a complex process of symbolic displacement', the domestic domain now symbolised the colonial frontier (Schwarz 1999: 206), rendering Worcester(shire) a final bastion of the historic (and fictional) white nation.

Such imagery reflects the insecurity surrounding national identity in this period, with concerns over race caught up with fears about Britain's seemingly diminishing international status: an 'essentially second-ranking state on the peripheries of Europe' or 'Italy with rockets' (Colley 1992: 312; Conekin et al 1999: 6). This is the backwards face of British modernity, looking to the past, but it was modern nonetheless, and bound up with contemporary issues; Schwarz argues that even such 'palpably conservative or racist manifestations of ethnic belonging...were, in their own way, modern' (1999: 191). The use of modern photographic effects or contemporary styling on some of the covers featuring the classic image of Worcester cathedral visually supports this claim to being modern (a/w 1965; S/S 1966; a/w 1967; S/S 1969). These covers also highlight that county or provincial identification did not simply equate to being traditional or old fashioned. The Autumn/Winter 1963 cover reinforces this duality. The image shows a woman leafing through Kays. She is wearing modern clothing (a turtleneck jumper and shift dress) and the large picture window behind her signals contemporary domestic architecture; through the window, we can of course see the River Severn and Worcester Cathedral.

These modern touches did not undermine the overall aura of timelessness, which in itself served a clear contemporary agenda. By evoking either a time before living memory or a hazy sense of enduring history, the covers bypassed the conflicts and divisions that characterise modern society. Such portrayals of an idealised, almost mythical world allowed an imagined belonging for a wide range of customers, thus intimating that Kays is the catalogue for them regardless of gender or social class (albeit not race). However, while at least in part a marketing strategy, these covers were not purely about commercial efforts to attract a broad customer base. Genuine pride was another factor. Although local identities dwindle in significance by the nineteenth century (Colley, 1992), the regional pride exhibited on the Kays covers links the Catalogue to a wider post-war provincial renaissance. The 1950s and 60s witnessed what Brian Harrison calls 'a broad-based revival in non-metropolitan culture', seen in regional television and theatre as well as literature (Harrison 2009: 168). Similar vitality is visible across other cultural sites too (Conekin, 2003; Wildman, 2012). The sheer extent of emphasis on Worcester(shire), alongside the positive promotion of the wider region that the covers gave, suggests that this discourse influenced the catalogue's creators.

If representations of Worcester(shire) in Kays express one particular version of modernity, a wholly different one is apparent in depictions of London, notwithstanding parallel themes evident in both. For a start, portrayals of the capital are far less unified compared to images of the local region; there is more variety and ambiguity surrounding the metropolis. This reflects the diverse cultural imaginings of the capital. Whereas the cultural revolution view of the 1960s positions London as an icon of British modernity in a very specific way, as the epitome of the 'Swinging' scene, Mort highlights that there were different versions of the city at work in the post-war decades (Mort, 2006; Mort, 2007). Findings from Kays support this assertion, as demonstrated by images of Savile Row compared to those of Swinging London.

In 1965 and 1968, Kay & Co offered a range of suits 'styled' in Savile Row, the home of a 'great tradition' of men's tailoring (S/S 1968: 376). The inclusion of a distinctive London road sign stating 'City of Westminster / Savile Row' reinforced the link between the street and the metropolis (S/S 1965: 360; S/S 1968: 376). This was an exclusively masculine image of the city. Despite the rise in women's employment during the post-war decades, there was no icon of female professional identity in widespread circulation and hence no way of depicting women in the masculine uniform domain of Savile Row. This endorsement was partly about symbolic capital, adding prestige to the suits featured: 'Let's face it – a Savile Row styled suit stands out in a crowd like a Rolls Royce in the local car park' (S/S 1965: 360). However, it was also in tune with the post-war rhetoric of egalitarianism, making an unaffordable luxury product more easily available to the masses: 'Now Kays can offer you just that' – the equivalent of a Rolls Royce (S/S 1965: 360). Whether one views this as democratisation or inauthenticity depends on one's perspective.

At the same time, the catalogue featured another class discourse in relation to the capital. During the 1950s and 60s, there was not so much a move to classlessness as a reconfiguration of social class. This is evident in trends such as increased social mobility (encapsulated in the figure of the grammar school boy) and the re-appraisal of working-class life, whether that be social investigators' celebration of so-called traditional communities or the valorisation of the working-class anti-hero in cultural works such as *Room at the Top* and *Look Back in Anger*. In Kays, the two facets of Lybro men's clothing typify this reconfiguration, with the firm making clothing such as boilersuits for manual workers as well as manufacturing highly fashionable items such as hipster trousers (S/S 1965: 401-405, 420-421; S/S 1968: 433-437, 444-445).

The trendy Lybro garments appeared in Kays' representations of fashionable London. Although traditional styles of dress continued to feature throughout the decade, by 1965 the catalogue incorporated the modish styling associated with Swinging London fashions: turtleneck jumpers, winklepicker shoes, suits with slimmer fitting cuts (S/S 1965: 418-421). This continues in 1968, with hipster trousers featured (S/S 1968: 410-420, 433). As well as items with the 'look', the catalogues included references to specific places linked with Swinging London. In 1965, Piccadilly Circus appears as a backdrop (S/S 1965: 422). By 1968, Kays cites Carnaby Street, a Soho thoroughfare at the very heart of the Swinging London scene. With parallels to representations of Savile Row, these references include road sign photographs and a range 'Styled by Mr Stance of Carnaby Street' (S/S 1968: 362-363, 420, 433). Other signifiers of Swinging London featured too, such as the music programme *Ready, Steady, Go!*, aped in a double-page spread supposedly set in a television studio and with two headlines using the words 'ready steady go' and 'ready to go' (S/S 1965: 420-421).

These examples are indicative of the major changes taking place in menswear from the 1950s, with young men increasingly targeted as fashionable consumers (Mort, 1996). This focus specifically on the younger generation is critical. The alignment of youth and Swinging London is widely recognised, with this scene often credited as being a driving force behind the decade's so-called 'youthquake': Swinging London 'was perceived...to be taking a new international lead, especially in popular music, fashion and youth culture' (Thane, 2001: 354). This comment also underlines the importance of this scene in terms of international exchange. The thriving fields of music and fashion were central to the nation's cultural exports in the 1960s and played a vital role making Britishness fashionable. This is a different version of modernity to the one expressed via Kays' covers. Swinging London represented the forward face of British modernity, one that gazed outwards and to the future. It symbolised a confident, optimist nation engaging with and contributing to the world through its new role as the vanguard of popular culture – a means of retaining international prominence at a time when Britain's position in its traditional spheres of influence, such as economics and politics, was severely under strain. The centrality of youth reinforces this sense of breaking with the past, moving away from the world of one's parents; Swinging London was about a new generation, removed from its elders and looking forwards not back for its points of reference.

The accent on youth remained prominent in Kays' womenswear. The pages showing Swinging London clothing styles universally featured models who look to be in their teens or early twenties and are littered with captions such as '6 great young coats' (S/S 1968: 169). This emphasis on youth affected ideals of female appearance. As Carol Dyhouse observes, 'the glamorous sophisticate was out of fashion as swinging dolly birds and flower children took centre stage, and haute couture gave way to Carnaby Street' (2010: 5). Swinging London was a world in which there was no accommodation of older women. Actually, there was little space for any women, regardless of age. In the 'Ready steady go' spread, the main photograph includes two young women alongside the male models and they too are in outfits with a Swinging London vibe – sweaters and slacks. This example is, though, unusual. Unlike menswear, it is only in 1968 that there are womenswear pages dedicated to Swinging London style items such as mini-skirts, hipster trousers and military-style coats (S/S 1968: 152-183).

Moreover, compared to the very specific linkages to Swinging London evident on some of the menswear pages, representations of this geo-cultural scene in relation to womenswear were far more generic. A 1968 double-page spread of Mary Quant clothing illustrates this. Although her designs 'epitomized young British fashion in "Swinging London"' (O'Hara Callan 1998: 194), there are no metropolitan references in the shoot; instead it has an orange studio backdrop punctuated by Quant's signature daisies (S/S 1968: 6-7). The other womenswear shoot featuring this style of clothing is similarly generic. Several of the pages have a musical theme under the headline 'What to wear for the Big!! [sic] Summer parade', but there are no explicit links to Swinging London's vibrant music scene (S/S 1968: 174-177). This is in stark contrast to the equivalent menswear and its clear positioning in terms of the capital's geography.

Why is this the case? Why do we see icons of Swinging London in the menswear pages but not the women's? The answer lies in the multifaceted reputation of the metropolis. While the city had positive connotations of vibrancy and style, many also regarded it as a morally ambiguous place. Prostitution and other more recent manifestations of the sex trade such as the strip club tarnished the reputation of those areas that also happened to be associated with Swinging London, namely Soho (Mort 2006; Mort 2007; Bartley and Gwinnett, 2001). What is more, such perceptions were highly gendered: the capital was a site of sexual for danger for women. This reflects the persistence of the double standard. For example, many still considered premarital sexual activity to be more acceptable for men than for women (Summerfield, 1994). Such attitudes indicate the relative freedom granted to men, while women remained subject to moral regulations despite significant landmarks in the history of sexuality during this decade, such as the arrival of the birth control pill (1963) and the Abortion Act (1967).

There was a racial element to this too. Although the only minority ethnic model in the sample appeared in the Mary Quant shoot (S/S 1968: 6-7), images of Swinging London echoed the discourses discussed in relation to Kays covers. Notably, fears about interracial sex grew as increasing numbers of non-white men migrated to the capital. Soho's 'longstanding associations with foreign bodies and spaces' (Mort 2007: 48) meant that the district's reputation was entwined not just with sex, but a heavily racialised image of sex that remained highly controversial. It seems, therefore, that Kay & Co were reluctant to show women in locations explicitly associated with Swinging London because of such sexual undertones: for every Mary Quant, there was a Christine Keeler; for every hip chick shopping on Carnaby Street, there was a Soho stripper. As a result, within the geographical imagination found in Kays, women occupy a marginal position in relation to both representations of Savile Row and Swinging London. This marginality insinuates that they do not really belong in the capital. However, such liminality and exclusion was not characteristic of Kays as a whole. In images of other locations, women featured far more prominently, as the next section explores.

Going abroad: representations of foreign holidays

Of those covers that did not feature Worcester or the surrounding area, two showed women in what appeared to be a non-British setting. Both related to photo shoots within the respective catalogue. In one, the model wears a Jackie Kennedy-esque shift dress and there is an enormous globe in the background. Inside, it is revealed that the setting is the New York World's Fair and the woman pictured is 'Top American model' Jan Rylander (S/S 1964: 4-5). While highly evocative of a certain kind of early- to mid-1960s style (think *Mad Men*), this particular image and the related shoot were not typical in Kays. The catalogue contained few visual representations of places as far afield as the US. Overall, images of international locations in womenswear and menswear were less Caribbean and more Costa Brava. Furthermore, such images were mostly generic depictions of hot and sunny places with a Mediterranean vibe rather than being specific, named places. Their purpose was to convey a sense of being on holiday rather than being concerned with the exact location.

The other cover showing a woman in an apparently foreign setting exemplifies this genre of picture. The cover is dominated by a head-and-shoulders shot of the model with a clear, bright blue sky behind her (S/S 1968). On the left, there is a narrow, soft focus photograph of several boats moored in a row. The photograph's hazy quality is purposeful. Firstly, the indistinctness contrasts with the bold sharpness and clarity of the main image, reinforcing that the focus is, literally, on the woman and not the place. Secondly, it reiterates that the specific place is not important. The boats could be gondolas, making the scene Venice, but one cannot quite tell. Nevertheless, the photograph is clear enough to signal plainly that the location is abroad. Other details further transmit a Mediterranean holiday atmosphere: the model's tanned skin and sun-kissed blond hair are catching the light; the title banner is a sand colour; the company's 'K' logo is orange and positioned like the sun, surrounded by yellow rays.

This image is far from unique. In 1965, one similarly characteristic shot shows three women on a balcony with sandstone buildings in the background; Blackpool it is not. In case the imagery is not obvious enough, an item caption makes the connotations explicit: 'Jaunty Blazer Suit with a carefree holiday air' (S/S 1965: 18-19). It is perhaps unsurprising to find holiday locations in two Spring/Summer catalogues, as such backdrops are a suitable seasonal setting for the clothing. However, the prevalence of 'foreign holiday' imagery indicates that it has meaning far beyond being merely an appropriate milieu for summer clothes. The main photo shoot in both 1965 and 1968 uses such a setting, and equates to approximately forty and seventy pages respectively, all in a prominent position at the front of the catalogue. Similar backdrops also appear on later pages. No other location receives anywhere near this degree of representation. This raises the question why is the world of foreign holidays so significant in Kays?

Part of the reason is that the inclusion of women in such settings is relatively unproblematic. Whereas representations of Swinging London carried undertones of sexual danger for women because of the seedy side of the capital's reputation, the holiday scenes appear as a safe space free from moral hazards. In 1965, for example, the shoot is headlined 'For the great day...and going away' and opens with a bride getting into a wedding car (S/S 1965: 2). Although there are no male models pictured, this depiction constructs the photographic subjects as married women holidaying with their husbands, therefore legitimising their presence abroad and eschewing any suggestion of transgressive behaviour. In contrast, the 'Kays beach companions' page in menswear is more sexually suggestive, featuring a female model alongside men in trunks (S/S 1965: 331).

Again, this construct hints at the continued double standard, although there are indications of changing attitudes towards women's sexual behaviour later in the decade. The Autumn/Winter 1966 cover has an illustration of Worcester Cathedral inset at the top, but the main image intimates heterosexual romance: it shows a young couple, smiling at one another and holding hands, apparently alone in a seemingly isolated alpine-type scene. Even more notably, in a gender reversal of 'Kays beach companions', one particular 'foreign holiday' photograph in 1968 shows two models surrounded by four sailors gazing at them adoringly (S/S 1968: 123). This remains carefully tempered; the women are in a pair, not alone, and both look straight at the camera, not back at the sailors. Despite this moral inference, the shot's playfulness evokes the freedom that holidays signify. They are a time and a place where the usual constraints do not limit behaviour quite as much as they do at home. Acknowledgment of this position in Kays through the hint of holiday romance indicates a definite shift in moral and social outlooks.

Other differences are apparent in representations of the foreign holiday too. Although the shoots showed only white models, there is variety in terms of age, with images including apparently middle-aged women (usually defined as forty to sixty-five). Again, this is more noticeable in 1968. The 1965 'Summer pretty!' spread featured a middle-aged model in summer dresses shot against a studio background (S/S 1965: 52-53). By 1968, comparable shoots were located in foreign settings similar to other holiday scenes in the Catalogue (S/S 1968: 50-65). This representation may have been a marketing ploy. Flattering images of middle-aged women that are barely distinguishable from pictures of younger models not only suggest that Kay & Co cater for a broad age range, they indicate an attempt to attract older customers. Unlike representations of Swinging London, a scene that incorporated only the younger generation (and more specifically younger men), the imaginary world of foreign holidays was more inclusive. This extended to embracing women who wore larger clothes sizes, with bigger size often conflated with older age. The headline 'Elegance in the larger sizes', for example, appeared on a page showing middle-aged models (S/S 1968: 60). Again, this position contrasts with the exclusions surrounding Swinging London, where the model Twiggy literally embodied the fashionable look and the desirable qualities of thinness and youth were inextricably linked.

Of course, this construct is about representation and not reality. Foreign travel was becoming more widespread but still was not a common experience; by 1968, only a tenth of British adults were holidaying abroad (Harrison, 2009). As a result, imaginings of foreign locations could retain an almost dreamlike quality in a way that all-too-familiar London, besmirched by reality, could not. Crucially, the Mediterranean-esque images typical in Kays were not too far removed from the aspirations and potential reach of the catalogue's working-class and lower-middle class customers. Whereas the unusual cover featuring the New York World's Fair evoked the world of the international jet set, the characteristic images speak of charter flights and package holidays. This is not to deny the symbolic capital of such depictions. It is simply to highlight that the holiday world in Kays was not an elitist form of foreign travel. Rather, it was an alternative conception of post-war British modernity that not only looked forwards and outwards, but also incorporated those excluded from other visions.

The range of styles featured further emphasises the extent to which the Catalogue's world of foreign holidays was an inclusive vision of modernity. This is most evident in 1968, when more pages show this kind of backdrop. Many of these featured older styles of dress, such as smart coats and tailored, knee-length skirts worn with pearls and gloves, and both men's and women's knitwear has a sunny coastal background (S/S 1968: 104-119, 400-403). These more traditional items continued to be popular and while they were not overtly modern, Kay & Co incorporated them into a modern setting. Such items often appeared alongside clothing more commonly associated with late 1960s fashions, such as short dresses in bold patterns and bright colours. However, even these latter garments are stylistically different to the clothes in the Swinging London-related shoots. They have a late 1960s look, but are not examples of high fashion. They too are modern, but a different kind of modern, albeit with overlaps. For instance, the Mary Quant mini-dresses were 34½ to 35½ inches long, whereas the Kay & Co short dresses that appear a couple of pages later against a foreign holiday backdrop ranged between 36 and 40 inches in length (S/S 1968: 6-7, 10-11).

Worlds within *Kays*

This imagined world of foreign holidays was prevalent in Kays because it was such a malleable vision, relatively unhindered by realism thanks to both an emphasis on atmospheric qualities rather than identifiable locations and the relatively limited number of Brits holidaying abroad. Such backdrops became even more widely used in 1968, a time when other versions of modernity in circulation were often too circumscribed. Representations of foreign holidays offered an alternative, allowing Kay & Co to cater for different customer tastes and incorporate a range of demographics. Unlike representations of Swinging London, there was no inherent generation divide or exclusivity around age. The images also expressed a version of modernity that the masses could aspire to, even if they could not quite access at that time. Rather than being an elitist interpretation of international travel, it was imagery in tune with the affluent society and changing notions of social class. Moreover, Kay & Co could easily show women in foreign holiday locations, again in contrast to the Swinging London scene. Within these portrayals, there were indications of changing attitudes to women's sexuality but there was still no suggestion of a professional identity for women, with holidays being a time of leisure and not work.

This relative inclusiveness allowed Kay & Co to appeal to a broad customer base, as they tried to do with representations of Worcester(shire) as well. Whereas the latter drew on the past and an insular understanding of national identity, foreign holidays symbolised an outwards gaze. These images show Brits engaging with the wider world, suggesting a sense of positivity and confidence about the country's global position. This open outlook is also about looking to the future, a nation moving forward and forging a new role for itself. Such symbolism reiterates the complex intertwining of time and place, both in the catalogue and more widely. The symbolic geography in Kays has a clear temporal dimension, with certain locations (namely Worcester and the surrounding region) allied with history (a semi-mythical past) and others associated with the future. Swinging London represents one expression of this alliance, and foreign holidays another. Nonetheless, holiday imagery reinforces the ambiguities surrounding national identity. Whilst seemingly confident, this new role is about tourism, essentially an individual engagement. It is not a collective contribution, as in the cultural exports of Swinging London. It is a role for British people, not the British nation. As well as reflecting increasing individualism and the growth of an affluent, leisured society, this role signals the continued uncertainty about post-war Britain's international position and status.

Furthermore, the bright sunshine belies the numerous tensions inherent within representations of foreign holidays. By shifting the focus away from the domestic frontier, these images avoided allusions to the end of empire and the psychic effect of this. They also bypassed reference to the rising levels of immigration to Britain, a growing cause of tension in this period. In addition, the concentration on Mediterranean-style settings minimised references to the US. Acknowledgement that the former colony had gone on to surpass Britain as the preeminent global influence, even in the cultural sphere where the Swinging London scene had achieved some success in carving out a new understanding of national identity, could therefore be evaded. At the same time, however, images of foreign holidays remained vague enough to circumvent both memories of the relatively recent war fought on European soil and the thorny issue of Britain's two failed bids to enter the European Economic Community.

Thus we see that the most accommodating versions of modernity in Kays, those connected to Worcester(shire) and to foreign holidays, have strong elements of fantasy to them: a reliance on a mythical past or a dream of an imaginary place abroad. Between them, they capture the Janus-face of post-war British modernity, looking backwards and forwards. All three competing representations of place, and the expressions of modernity linked with them, demonstrate the tensions and difficulties facing Britain in trying to negotiate new understandings of national identity in the post-1945 period and generate a new role for the nation on the world stage. The Swinging London scene offered some possibilities in this respect. However, this ~~a~~ version of modernity centred on a small geographical area. The sexual and racial connotations of this place, particularly Soho, restricted the popular appeal of the discourse. In addition, this vision only really incorporated young men. It was too exclusive to generate a widespread narrative of national purpose, even though this is the image of 1960s Britain that we have come to remember.

This exploration has shown that as historians we need to consider imaginings of other places, and therefore continue to move beyond the Cultural Revolution model of the 1960s if we are to fully capture the nuances and complexities of this undeniably transitional decade. It was a time when the nation's powerful past cast a shadow over attempts to deal with a plethora of socio-cultural, economic and political shifts, from the increasing marginalisation of older generations and changes in women's roles to the legacy of empire, tensions surrounding race and efforts to decipher our position within Europe. The worlds within Kays – regional, metropolitan, international – provide an insight into contemporary understandings of these challenges and how they were interpreted. They are issues that we are continuing to wrestle with today.

References

Kays catalogue spring/summer and Autumn/Winter 1960 – 1969.
Woman week ending September 27 1969.
Anthony, S., and Mansell, J.G. (2012) Introduction: The documentary film movement and the spaces of British identity. *Twentieth Century British History*, 23 (1), pp. 1-11.
Bartley, P. and Gwinnett, B. (2001) Prostitution. In Zweiniger-Bargielowska, I. (ed.) *Women in twentieth-century Britain.* Harlow, Pearson, pp. 214-228.
Colley, L. (1992) Britishness and otherness: an argument. *Journal of British Studies*, 31 (4), 309-329.
Conekin, B. (2003) *Autobiography of a nation.* Manchester, University of Manchester Press.
Conekin, B., Mort, F. and Waters, C. (1999) Introduction. In: Conekin, B., Mort, F. and Waters, C. (eds.) *Moments of modernity – reconstructing Britain 1945-1964.* London, Rivers Oram Press, pp. 1-21.
Dyhouse, C. (2010) *Glamour – women, history, feminism.* London, Zed Books.
Giles, J. (2004) *The parlour and the suburb – domestic identities, class, femininity and modernity.* Oxford, Berg.
Harrison, B. (2009) *Seeking a role – the United Kingdom 1951-1970.* Oxford, Oxford University Press.
Heathcote, D. (2004) *Sixtiesstyle – home decoration and furnishings from the 1960s.* Middlesex, Middlesex University Press.
Langhamer, C. (2005) The meanings of home in postwar Britain. *Journal of Contemporary History*, 40 (2), 341-362.
Lien, M. (2000) Imagined cuisines: 'nation' and 'market' as organising structures in Norwegian food marketing. In: Jackson, P., Lowe, M., Miller, D., and Mort, F. (eds.) *Commercial cultures – economies, practices, spaces.* Oxford, Berg, pp. 153-174.
Marwick, A. (1998) *The sixties – cultural revolution in Britain, France, Italy and the United States, c1958-c1974.* Oxford, Oxford University Press.
Matless, D. (2012) Accents of landscape in GPO country: the Horsey Mail, 1938. *Twentieth Century British History*, Vol 23(1), 57-59.
Mort, F. (2007) Striptease: the erotic female body and live sexual entertainment in mid-twentieth-century London. *Social History*, 32 (1), 27-53.
Mort, F. (2006) Scandalous events: metropolitan culture and moral change in post-Second World War London. *Representations*, 93 (1), 106-137.
Mort , F. (1996) *Cultures of consumption – masculinities and social space in late twentieth-century Britain.* London, Routledge.
O'Hara Callan, G. (1998) *The Thames and Hudson dictionary of fashion and*

fashion designers. 2nd edition. London, Thames and Hudson.
Schwarz, B. (1999) Reveries of race: the closing of the imperial moment. In: Conekin, B., Mort, F. and Waters, C. (eds.) *Moments of modernity – reconstructing Britain 1945-1964*. London, Rivers Oram Press, pp. 189-207.
Strub, W. (2008) The clearly obscene and the queerly obscene: heteronormativity and obscenity in Cold War Los Angeles. *American Quarterly*, 60 (2), 373-398.
Summerfield, P. (1994) Women in Britain since 1945: companionate marriage and the double burden. In: Obelkevich, J., and Catterall, P. (eds.), *Understanding post-war British society*. London, Routledge, pp. 58-72.
Thane, P. (2001), *Cassell's companion to twentieth-century Britain*. London, Cassell & Co.
Thomas, N. (2002) Challenging myths of the 1960s: the case of student protest in Britain. *Twentieth Century British History*, 13 (3), 277-297.
Waters, C. (1997) "Dark Strangers" in our midst: discourse of race and nation in Britain, 1947-1963. *Journal of British Studies* 36 (2), 207-238.
Wildman, C. (2012) A *City Speaks*: The projection of civic identity in Manchester. *Twentieth Century British History*, Vol 23(1), 80-99.
Wilson, E. (1980) *Only halfway to paradise – women in postwar Britain: 1945-1968*. London, Tavistock Publications.

// Chapter 5 //
Resistance to Commodified Girlhood in Two Young Adult Novels: Eileen Fairweather's *French Letters* and Jacqueline Wilson's *Waiting for the Sky to Fall*

Kate Flynn

The purpose of this essay is to analyse how mail order catalogues and comparable consumer publications are depicted by two teen novels. My analysis assumes that, by examining the fictionalised counterparts of Kays catalogues, we will glean new understanding of the resonances of these catalogues in the wider culture. The first book I will discuss is *French Letters* (Fairweather, 1987), a comedic epistolary novel in which the protagonist becomes infatuated with her French pen friend. I will then examine *Waiting for the Sky to Fall* (Wilson, 1983), a social realist story that follows the diverging interests of two working class sisters. Both texts feature scenes in which perusing consumer publications is associated with feelings of inadequacy. My argument is that these scenes express anxiety about the commodification of girlhood.

Before proceeding, I will define key terms to aid clarity. When I use the phrase "commodified girlhood", I mean a feminine ideal that girls are encouraged to fulfil through buying material goods. The phrase "consumer publications" refers to texts where the implied reader is engaged with purchasing choices. That engagement may be as a customer, or alternatively, as someone who fantasises about consumption without necessarily buying. Such publications include mail order catalogues, but also other periodicals such as fashion magazines.

Fairweather and Wilson advance different strategies for resisting commodified girlhood, rooted in different understandings of how teenagers engage with consumer publications. In *French*, catalogue shopping dupes impressionable girls into restrictive gender roles. This feminist stance is consistent with the values of Livewire, Fairweather's publisher. Livewire is a teen imprint of The Women's Press who, then as now, promoted new feminist fiction by women writers (Murray 2004: 73-75) *French*'s protagonist, Maxine, tries to fulfil a range of mutually exclusive feminine ideals through her combination of catalogue purchases. Her failure is personally humiliating as well as at a financial cost she can't afford. The text implies that resisting commodified girlhood consists in recognising consumer publications as exploitative.

Waiting, on the other hand, suggests that consumer imagery can be repurposed for subversive play. I interpret the text's teen narrator, Katherine, as a "bricoleur" of consumer publications. According to Claude Lévi-Strauss (1966), the bricoleur is a figure who speaks "through the medium of things; giving an account of his personality and life by the choices he makes between the limited possibilities. The bricoleur may not ever complete his purpose but he always puts himself into it" (p.21). Lévi-Strauss goes on to state that the bricoleur does not subordinate tasks "to the availability of raw materials and tools conceived and procured for the purpose of the project" (p.17). This definition of the bricoleur can be helpfully applied to *Waiting*; as I will show, Katherine treats consumer publications as "raw material" for inspiring imaginative games rather than making purchases.

Note that both novels are implicitly critical of consumer publications. During my initial literature search, no young adult novel unambiguously celebrated the catalogue shopping experience. Portrayals of catalogue shopping were also far rarer, in general, than portrayals of high street sprees and trips to the mall. High street shopping also features in *French* and *Waiting*, but is primarily referred to for its shortcomings. Both texts depict young girls who are excluded from high street shopping by limited financial means and parental strictures. As Maxine and Katherine's negative experiences on the high street contextualise their responses to consumer publications, I dedicate part of my analysis to the portrayal of brick and mortar shops. The frustrations of aspiring to a lifestyle one cannot attain will then be shown to inhere within an ostensibly more accessible site of consumerism and gender conformity: catalogues and magazines, obtained via older relatives or acquaintances.

"The Right Combination"? Emulating Consumer Images

Before criticising mail order catalogues, *French* provides a context for their appeal by emphasising the elitism of face-to-face retail. Maxine Harrison is a fourteen year old girl who lives in Hornsey, a district of London (p.1). Her family has a low income: her mother works in a chip shop (p.7), and her father, whose class position informs his political stance as a socialist (p.9), is a bus conductor (p.3). When Maxine's penfriend, a boy named Jean, announces his intention to visit England, she immediately fears that she hasn't "got ANYTHING to wear" (p.73). As an inhabitant of the capital, she has theoretical access to a wide range of shops, but she finds the attitudes of retail staff humiliating: she agrees with her sister's assertion that "it's something to do with my age. And my accent. And my clothes" (p.79).

The first example of this humiliation occurs early in the novel, setting the tone for Maxine's subsequent forays into clothes shopping. Mrs Harrison takes Maxine out to buy a new school uniform. Maxine anticipates that they will attract unwanted attention because Mrs Harrison is on a break from work and is still wearing her overalls. She emphasises the mortification of "going into a dead posh shop like Banhams The School Outfitters with your mum in purple nylon" (p.7). The shop assistant's reaction vindicates Maxine's initial suspicions rather than positioning them as adolescent self-consciousness. In a letter to her best friend, Maxine describes her indignation when the assistant obliquely comments on their ability to pay:

> "And will Madam be paying by *voucher*?" Vouchers – ?! You know, like we were so dead poor we were on the dole or something. Luckily Mum didn't hear, she was still too busy bargain hunting on the knicker counter. She'd have been ever so hurt. It was for her sake really that I decided to put that snotty woman down. You'd have been proud of me. I put on my best posh voice and snarled that of course we weren't on vouchers. (p.7)

The contrast between Maxine's denial that they are poor, and her mother hunting for knicker bargains, is a source of intended humour; but this paragraph also fulfils the more serious function of marking shops as a hostile environment for people on a limited income. The assistant's insinuations are presented as a common strategy for undermining shoppers. Maxine will later comment, "You know how sniffy those boutiques are when they can tell you're broke? I mean, the snotty way they say 'Can I Help You Madam?" when what they really mean is 'Sod Off'?" (p.61).

Elitist attitudes are held by fellow shoppers as well as members of shop staff. Maxine laments, on a later trip, that the layout decisions made by retailers encourage shoppers to scrutinise each other:

> In one boutique I found a lovely size fourteen dress that I was sure would fit but they'd only got one of those big cattle-barn places for trying things on. You know, where all the other girls look down their noses at you because your underwear's old and you can't do up the zips. (p.61)

The text suggests that changing rooms enable judgements to be made about strangers' clothing, and also their bodies. Maxine has previously described herself as "fat" (p.22) and "a big bruiser" (p.26); the high street's poor provision of clothes on which she can "do up the zips" heightens the potential for unwanted attention. Shops are thus portrayed as unwelcoming places for girls who do not comply with a narrowly defined feminine bodily ideal.

This is not the only gendered barrier to Maxine's use of brick and mortar shops. Mrs Harrison restricts Maxine's unaccompanied shopping trips, because of Maxine's perceived vulnerability as a minor and a girl. Maxine remarks, of a renowned shopping area in London's West End, that "Mum never even lets me up Oxford Street on my own. She's got it into her head that drug pushers jump out of doorways and stick needles into your arm to get you hooked (HONESTLY!)" (p.72). Despite Maxine's scorn, the text legitimates Mrs Harrison's view in a scene where Maxine goes shopping alone and experiences sexual street harassment:

> ...I went down Wood Green, window shopping. Then this man started walking beside me muttering. I thought he was just another loony, but then he asked if I was wearing tights, or stockings. (p.61)

She succeeds in deterring him by threatening to call the police, but the scene contributes to an overall impression of public spaces – including shops – as hazardous for young girls.

When the novel first refers to catalogues, a number of their features implicitly counter these barriers to Maxine's enjoyment of shopping. At a financial level, the possibility of paying by instalments (p.80) is suited to Maxine's meagre, and slowly accumulated, income as a babysitter (p.67), as well as to Mrs Harrison's willingness to bank her tips before the payment date is due (p.66). The text positions this method as an attractive option, relative to the high street where Mrs Harrison frets that prices are higher (p.7) and payment must be made upfront. But in addition to the practical advantages of spreading out payments, consulting catalogues does not involve the sense of intimidation Maxine has come to expect when purchasing clothes.

Mrs Harrison's friend, Linda, is a catalogue agent, and Maxine initially views catalogues as serving a social, rather than economic function: "I don't think that Linda ever sells anything from those catalogues of hers, it's just that humping them around gives her and Mum and all the other women a great excuse to gas" (p.35). The circulation of the catalogue amongst friends decreases the likelihood of humiliation that Maxine associates with brick and mortar shops.

Furthermore, because the catalogue is consulted in the home, Maxine occupies a stronger position for influencing her mother's spending priorities. Unlike their earlier trip for a school uniform, which was subject to distractions and deadlines because Mrs Harrison was shopping in her break, the catalogue can be consulted repeatedly over time, granting Maxine extended opportunities to inveigle a share of family finances:

> Mum found me flicking through it. I wasn't really putting it on, honest. I was just going 'Ooh' and 'Aah' and 'Look at those lovely clothes!' and sniffing and crying a bit. Suddenly Mum said, 'For God's sake, get out of that school blazer, I'm sick of the sight of it,' and got on the phone to Linda and told her to sign me up for Eighty Quids' Worth of Clothes!!!! Great! (p.80)

The repetition of "and", the allusions to manipulation in "sniffing and crying", followed by the suddenness of Mrs Harrison's response, all indicate that Maxine is maintaining an ongoing commentary to erode her mother's resistance. At this stage the pleasure in fantasies of consumption are foregrounded: the multiple exclamation marks, and the use of emphatic capitalisation, both convey Maxine's enthusiasm. But up to this point, Maxine's participation in the market has been largely theoretical. Once Maxine's access to new material goods is assured, the text's anxieties concerning consumerism, particularly as a site of gender conformity, become more apparent.

Maxine considers how she might emulate the different models of femininity showcased by the catalogue, and finds herself bewildered. To amplify her confusion, the portability of catalogues means that she is counselled by a far wider range of people than would accompany her on a high street shopping trip. She receives advice from not only her mother, her sister and her best friend, but her father, her best friend's brother, and the next door neighbours:

> Mum said I should get something classic but Sue said that meant boring. Sue said I should get something trendy but Mum said that meant rubbish. Imelda said get something romantic but Frankie said that meant sexless. Frankie said get something low cut but Mrs M. told him to go pray to Mary, Queen of Virgins. Dad just said, "Bugger it, look at the interest rates." (p.81)

The syntax varies little over the course of the paragraph – there are four compound sentences, each one comprised of two instances of reported speech, with the repetition of "but" emphasising the lack of consensus. One effect of the unvarying sentence structure is to suggest that the choices themselves have little meaning for Maxine. Each option, whether "classic", "boring", "trendy", "rubbish", "romantic", sexless", or "low cut", is simply one amongst many confusing possibilities. The pairs of contrasting demands encapsulate some of the difficulties of complying with feminine ideals through purchasing choices: if you satisfy one ideal, you must fail to meet another. Maxine's indecision over what clothes she should buy is therefore engaged with conflicting social expectations of how girls should look and behave.

Maxine's response to these limited binaries is to listen to the positive recommendations, and ignore the negative. She tries to make purchases in "the right combination" (p.91) to fulfil all the expectations made of her:

> I got in a real panic and now I've ended up making everyone happy except me. I ordered the navy blue cardi that Mum said wouldn't date, the orange lurex top that Frankie liked, the green and white spotted trousers that Sue chose, and some white high heels with sparkly bows that Imelda said were dead feminine. Now I'm worried they won't all go together. Amanda said I should have stuck to my own taste, but I've never had enough money to work out what that is. (p.81)

The references to "panic" and being "worried" convey that Maxine's fantasy of consumption has become a source of distress rather than pleasure. While her attempts to please everybody are partly responsible for her sense of unhappiness, her naiveté as a consumer means she has no feasible means of distinguishing one piece of advice from another. Maxine's exchange with Amanda implies that expressions of individuality, and not just compliance with social expectation, are commodified: from Maxine's perspective, one's "own taste" is learned through the very practice of buying goods and is dependent on your financial means.

The impossibility of emulating every model of femininity in the catalogue is reinforced when Jean arrives in England and Maxine wears her new clothes for the first time. At this point the negative portrayal of catalogue shopping segues, problematically, into mockery of Maxine as a catalogue shopper. The text's movement between emphasising the conflicting demands on Maxine and ridiculing her selection of clothes replicates a tension in contemporaneous feminist activism and ideology. (For a summary of the contradictory feelings towards the treatment of fashion in feminist publishing and women's collectives, including collectives Fairweather contributed to such as Spare Rib, see Beckingham 2005: pp87-108.) Namely, *French* critiques the dictates of fashion as misogynist, by attacking an individual who – through a variety of sociocultural constraints and personal desires – tries to comply with feminine ideals. The reader is invited to laugh at Maxine when she writes the following account of Jean's arrival in another letter to her best friend:

> He looked like a *real* man. You'd have loved it. It was just like a scene from one of those pink Romance books...
>
> *The look he gave me was scorching. His eyes flickered over me, up and down, up and down, as he inspected me from head to foot. He couldn't take his eyes off me. I could see he was smitten.*
>
> *I felt so chic in my new clothes. They had only arrived that morning. I hadn't been sure that the green and white trousers and orange lurex top were the right combination, but now I felt more sure than I had felt of anything in my life. Beneath Jean's gaze I felt ravishing.*
>
> *In his hand lay a photograph. As he looked from it to me and back again his lip curled in a way that was devastatingly manly, devastatingly French. Obviously he couldn't believe his luck that at last we had met in the flesh, and our dream had become reality.*
>
> *At last I silently nodded "yes" to his question. A look almost of pain crossed his face. Then, manfully, he fought back his desire* (p.91)

Maxine fantasises that the "chicness" of her purchases grant her a new identity as the romantic heroine. But there are indicators that Fairweather is deploying dramatic irony. Where Maxine reads Jean as "smitten" and holding back "desire", his reactions might equally signal disdain and disbelief. More overtly, the incongruity of "orange lurex" amongst the tropes of popular romance plays a key part in suggesting that Maxine is misreading the situation.

Sure enough: the passage is immediately followed by the railway porter mistaking her for a prostitute, and Jean commenting that "it wasn't surprising, given the way [she] was dressed" (p.93). Her new clothing is also physically uncomfortable in ways that, over the course of the day, fail to comply with her hopes of being "dead feminine" (p.81). In particular, she discovers the drawbacks of her new stilettos: "I'd never have bought these shoes if I'd been able to tell from the catalogue how high they are. I know that high heels are supposed to make your legs look slimmer, but what's the point if they're both in plaster?" (p.93). Her feet blister and bleed, and Jean complains that the sores look "disgusting" (p.100). Despite his vehement reaction, Maxine's persistent hope that the shoes lend her feminine allure is fuel for further dramatic irony; on Jean's last day, Maxine reflects, "I nearly didn't wear the heels to the station, but I couldn't resist giving Jean one last peek at my legs. I want him to feel sick as a pig about what he'll be missing" (p.110).

Fairweather's dramatic irony undermines the valorisation of the "dead feminine" that is central to Maxine's fantasies of consumption. Yet making Maxine the butt of the joke has the startling effect of repositioning the text as conduct fiction. Maxine's responsiveness to consumer images, and the ease with which she is conned as to what consumer choices can achieve, assume the status of an individual flaw once we begin to laugh at her. The solution to commodified girlhood is correspondingly centred on Maxine's individual actions. This involves Maxine rejecting the "dead feminine" by, for instance, reverting to "flatties" (p.110); and realising that despite the appeal of mail order catalogues, their commodification of girlhood primarily benefits the retailer.

Her realisation is prompted by a financial crisis. Near the novel's denouement, Maxine is forced to admit she cannot keep up with the payment schedule (p.111). Her parents are angered because they must settle the bill using money they had saved for Christmas (p.115). Maxine is able to re-earn their approval by securing a cleaning job which, though illegal due to her age, allows her to pay them back: "They're very pleased. Mum celebrated with Spanish Gut Rot and Dad patted me on the back and sang 'The Red Flag'" (p.117).

The tongue-in-cheek reference to Mr Harrison's socialist leanings might suggest that consumerism needs to be challenged systemically, through collective rather than individual action. But Maxine's new sense of class solidarity – which is also expressed by going on a May Day demonstration with her father (p.117) – arises *after* she has grown disillusioned with catalogue shopping, and emerges so close to the end of the text that her politicisation has very little narrative impact. Maxine's recognition that the catalogue is exploitative is instead closely tied to questions of morality – specifically the importance of thrift and developing a work ethic. At the last, *French* is a cautionary tale. Mr Harrison's recommendation to "Bugger it, look at the interest rates – the only piece of shopping advice Maxine originally ignored outright – is retrospectively positioned as the wisest counsel. The immediate way to resist commodified girlhood, Fairweather implies, is through old fashioned frugality.

"Playing Paper People:" Repurposing Consumer Images

Maxine's melding of images drawn from catalogue stock and popular romance novels is used for humorous effect in *French*. Yet it is interesting to note that, to paraphrase Lévi -Strauss, Maxine attempts to give an account of her life through the medium of things. For Fairweather, this process is part of the problem – telling one's life through things is precisely what commodified girlhood entails. But in *Waiting*, Wilson adopts an opposing stance: bricolage is a means of *resisting* commodified girlhood.

Waiting focuses on a tumultuous relationship between the narrator, fifteen year old Katherine Petworthy, and her younger sister, Nicola, who is thirteen. A rift develops between them because examination stress and Katherine's first romance disrupt a home life previously characterised by social isolation and imaginative play. One imaginative game is of particular interest here. Throughout childhood, Katherine has collected consumer images from publications such as pattern books and Sunday supplements, which promote lifestyles beyond her financial reach (pp.62-65). She combines scraps from these publications with her own drawings to create a game called "Paper People" (p.10). The game provides opportunities to alternately bond and argue with Nicola during play, and serves a second function in subverting consumer imagery that Katherine experiences as marginalising.

Before discussing the manner of that subversion, I will analyse Wilson's portrayal of brick and mortar shops as inaccessible to Katherine. Like Maxine, Katherine finds that her enjoyment of window shopping – regardless of the intention to buy – is hampered by fellow shoppers' responses to her current attire. In *Waiting* as in *French*, open plan changing rooms evoke a sense of being watched and judged: "I didn't really mind exposing my own childish chest, but I was terrified that they'd see my knickers. I only had ghastly grey school knickers or some ancient, floppy, white ones with baggy legs that I seemed to have been wearing most of my life" (p.31). Although shops are hostile environments for both Katherine and Maxine, Katherine cannot retreat, as Maxine does, into a domesticated, community-based and thus welcoming arena of catalogue shopping. Her constraints differ from Maxine's, despite their having limited financial resources in common, because Katherine's father asserts his patriarchal dominance through household economics to a far greater degree than Mr Harrison.

Mrs Petworthy, Katherine and Nicola all work in the family business, a provincial newsagent's owned by Mr Petworthy. This labour does not provide them with any financial freedom. Mr Petworthy assumes exclusive control of the family purse and pays low wages as an exercise in his authority. His wife is no more able to make independent purchases than their daughters. Katherine is conscious that her father treats his wife and children as equivalent in this regard:

> It was rarely any use going to Mum for money. Her house-keeping allowance was so meagre she couldn't make ends meet herself. Whenever things got desperate and we couldn't afford something we *had* to buy, the three of us had to go to Dad and plead. I couldn't bear the look on his face at these times. How could he triumph at such a degrading victory? (p.11)

Katherine is limited to making essential purchases, cannot make any purchases alone, and must do so with the expectation of paternal humiliation. Ironically, consumer publications are one product that is always at the disposal of the Petworthy women, at least in the form of magazines and newspapers; "counter copies" can be read "carefully" before sale in the shop (p.39).

As a consequence of Mr Petworthy's restrictions, both Katherine, and her mother, are heavily reliant on their ability to craft and repurpose items rather than purchase them. Katherine's clothes are usually made rather than bought; this causes ongoing unhappiness because Mrs Petworthy cannot afford high quality fabric, and instead buys "frightful, man-made, flimsy muck" (p.26). Nor can Mrs Petworthy sew well: "Mum was bad at dressmaking, even though she now used proper patterns instead of improvising from our Paper People fashion book" (p.26). Katherine states that bought clothes, even when they are "a bit garish and thrown together" would be preferable because they are at least made to an industry standard; they "all looked *right*" (p.30). The mockery of Maxine in *French* cannot occur in this context, because Maxine's own garish and thrown together outfit is beyond Katherine's reach.

Katherine's first excursions into making outfits for herself differ in approach from her mother's. Unlike the bricoleur, Mrs Petworthy *does* use "raw materials and tools conceived and procured for the purpose of the project" - but she fails to achieve the desired effect, Katherine re-purposes what she has available from "limited possibilities". She recognises that although she harbours fantasies of looking "grown-up, flamboyant, poised, sexy" (p.30) in a "white broderie anglaise blouse or the black trousers cut in the latest style" (p.30), this fantasy is not attainable. She aims at a "shabby and home-made" alternative which she nevertheless hopes is "interesting" and "art-studenty" (p.98). When she is asked out by her first boyfriend, she uses an old paint box for make up (p.40), fashions a hair ribbon into a necktie (p.40), and embroiders the collar of her school blouse with a daisy pattern so that she has something attractive to wear (p.98).

An itemisation of playthings in Katherine's room conveys that Katherine has grown up with the expectation of refashioning what she can get hold of. She states: "I didn't really have many toys left. Dad always said they were a waste of money" (p.12). Her possessions include a broken snowglobe once received as a gift (p.6); a doll's house that she made in primary school using cartons and cotton reels (p.12); and a fake fur muff that she pretends is "a small, brown animal" called Muffle (p.10).

Just as Katherine views bought clothes as the "right" sort of clothes, she looks on these makeshift items as inferior. Although she is well into adolescence, she continues to resent her former lack of toys. Her boyfriend's younger sister, seven year old Wendy, becomes a focus for jealous feelings – and when she is presented with the opportunity, Katherine rifles through Wendy's belongings:

> I was surprised by the vast number of her toys. She had a proper matching suite of bedroom furniture, but only half size, specially for a small girl. I sat down on the pink padded stool in front of her little dressing-table and touched her brush and comb set, her Pretty Peach talcum and skin perfume, her jewellery box. I opened it up and a tiny plastic ballet dancer started revolving to a tinkling distortion of the "Sugar Plum Fairy". Wendy had several bits of plastic rubbish, the bracelets and rings they give away free in girls' comics, but she had some real pieces too. (pp.172-173)

Objects which are "proper" and "real" can be read as objects which are *used for the intended purpose*, unlike Katherine's makeshift toys. The "rubbish" Katherine is quickest to dismiss is precisely the type of "free" give away she would be likely to encounter in the family newsagent's. Proper, real objects are *bought* – and this is underscored by Katherine naming the specific brand of talcum powder. At the same time the passage conveys a discomfort with the idea of numerous products intended "specially for a small girl." References to the "distortion" of the music box tune, and to the ballet dancer being made of "plastic", do not belong to the same lexical set as "proper" and "real." Rather the opposite. "Distortion" and "plastic" are both suggestive of artifice. The extreme femininity of the room – most notably, the "vast number" of toys modelled on adult women's accoutrements in a pinker, smaller scale – is closely entwined with a commodification of what a little girl should be.

Before leaving the room, Katherine "inevitably" reflects on "how Nicola and I would have liked to have had real jewellery, real perfume, real matching furniture, when we were Wendy's age" (pp.172-173). The preoccupation with "real" objects conveys Katherine's sense that her own childhood has been inadequate. This provides a context for Katherine's responses to consumer publications, which I will explore momentarily. While Maxine is duped into buying products that she cannot afford, and that cannot achieve all the feminine qualities she is encouraged to emulate, Katherine feels inadequate because she is never given the opportunity to buy. To extrapolate from Katherine's longing for "real" objects, Katherine implies she cannot be a "proper" or a "real" girl because the material goods which construct girlhood as cosseted and appearance-orientated are beyond her reach.

It is through the *repurposing* of consumer imagery, which Katherine engages in just as she repurposes everything else, that she is able to resist feelings of insecurity. The Paper People game allows Katherine to express her ambivalence towards commodified girlhood, as something she wants but resents for being unattainable. The first description of a Paper Person is comparable with Katherine's subsequent envy and disdain for Wendy as a similarly cosseted little girl:

> Nicola asked if she could have the book and cut out all the little fashion girls she could find with long, curly hair and party frocks. I watched her snip one particularly simpering specimen and decide to give her a personality. She became Patty Pert, eight years old, cosseted only daughter of Bert and Gert Pert, publican and wife. Patty was the doyen of her local dancing class, had once acted in a television commercial for toilet paper and was determined to further her career in show business.

Katherine clearly recognises which characteristics a "little fashion girl" should possess: "long, curly hair," "dancing" and a "career in show business." But the reference to Patty as "particularly simpering" and the implication she was previously unendowed with a personality show that this description is parodic. The tone is notably different from Maxine's delighted enthusiasm when she first browses the catalogue. Katherine has already identified that she cannot emulate "Patty Pert", and is accordingly scathing.

At other times, Katherine confers an intellectual life on the figures she and her sister cut out. She recounts that "my own paper people were glamorous women inappropriately christened Charlotte, Emily, Anne, Virginia, Sylvia, Marianne and Jane" (p.62). Bestowing the names of female authors and literary characters on her makeshift dolls allows Katherine to create a space for her interests that she doesn't see reflected in consumer publications. Equally, imbuing the Paper People game with literary rather than consumerist resonances allows her to legitimate a past-time she suspects is infantile and class inflected. Katherine fears that it is "abnormal" (p.10) for a fifteen year old to enjoy imaginary play. She is also aware that, as a scholarship student at a private school, her early reading history was very different from her classmates; "I'd found out at Lady Margaret Lancaster's that I'd been reading all the wrong books" (p.12). Her choice of literary names helps to assuage both insecurities, though only to a degree. She remarks that though she used to "enjoy the Paper People game", she has grown increasingly "ashamed" of playing (p.10). Her English teacher responds to this admission by drawing parallels between Katherine's modification of consumer images, and the imaginary games played by the Brontes, Eleanor Farjeon and Antonia Forest (p.10).

The allocation of literary names changes the discursive context of Katherine's "little fashion girls". Supplementing the game with visual images of her own making further allows Katherine to voice fears and to laugh at troubling scenarios in a safe context. The power of these scenarios is indicated by the fact Katherine has to draw them, because they have no equivalent in the representations of commodified girlhood she cuts up. Such fears include precisely the kind of sexual threat that hindered Maxine, in *French*, while high street shopping. Katherine recollects: "I made up a fumbly little man in a greasy raincoat to lurk near my paper ladies. I was rather fond of Mr Tremble but Nicola said he made her feel sick, and when he started to edge up to pretty Patty Pert she banished him to the back of the fashion book" (pp. 62-63). By creating Mr Tremble, Katherine imagines herself to be out of the reach of sexual assault, and is able to vicariously enact her hostility towards "pretty Patty Pert" at the same time.

This is not Mr Tremble's only purpose. Katherine resents the inadequacy she feels when looking at consumer publications' portrayal of happy family life – and young motherhood in particular. Katherine is actively hostile towards younger children, who she refers to as "little beasts" (p.25). She resents the expectation she should want to nurture them because she is female. When her school arranges for her to undertake work experience at a local nursery, some of these resentments become apparent in the Paper People Game. Together, Katherine and Nicola imagine a pregnancy for one of their paper women, and Mr Tremble enables Katherine to express discomfort with the scenario by making sinister jokes. "Who can the father be?" she asks. "Perhaps she was attacked in the school grounds by Mr Tremble" (p.25). She helps Nicola cut out a baby from the children's section of their pattern book, but as soon as Nicola extends the game into caring for the child – pretending to feed him and change his nasty little nappy" (p.25)– Katherine disengages. The game complies too closely with a feminine role that simultaneously horrifies Katherine and makes her feel inadequate; she is reminded that she is "useless with real flesh and blood children" (pp.25-26).

Katherine, unlike Maxine, is never held individually responsible for the impact consumer publications have upon her. Consequently there is no moral coda in *Waiting* as there is in *French*. The reader is left with the expectation that Katherine will persist in bricolating consumer imagery in her own emotional interests, given no change in her financial or familial circumstances. Although Katherine's re-working of consumer publications endows her with greater agency than Maxine appears to possess, the lack of anticipated change at the text's close is bleak. The final section of the book is, indeed, emphatic in its continued anxiety over commodified girlhood, as evidenced by the following scenes.

Katherine is reconciled with Nicola (p.203), through a crisis brought about by Katherine's poor examination results – but not before Nicola tries to run away (p.202). Significantly, Nicola conceals herself in the changing room of a department store at closing time, fantasising that she could "walk round all the departments and try on every single dress she fancied and play with all the toys and eat some of the cakes and sweets in the food department and then curl up in the great, showy, modern four-poster in Bedding" (p.202). The fantasy goes awry when the shop lights are turned out, and Nicola cowers in fear of the dark until a security guard hears her scream. This event, on the novel's penultimate page, leaves readers with a final image of the retail environment as a hostile one for young girls.

French and *Waiting* make very different assumptions about how teenage girls are effected by commodified girlhood, while sharing a conviction that consumer publications are one constituent in a harmful consumer culture. Both texts advance strategies for managing the effects of consumerism on young girls. But neither Fairweather nor Wilson ventures to suggest how the effects might be stopped at source. Here, they too, are in the dark.

References

Beckingham, C. (2005) *Is fashion a woman's right?* Brighton, Sussex Academic Press.

Fairweather, E. (1987) *French letters.* London, Livewire.

Lévi-Strauss, C. (1966) *The savage mind.* Trans. Weidenfeld, G. Chicago, The University of Chicago Press.

Murray, S. (2004) *Mixed media: Feminist presses and publishing politics.* London, Pluto Press.

Wilson, J. (1983) *Waiting for the sky to fall.* Oxford, Oxford University Press.

// Chapter 6 //
Catalogues, advertising, gender and the future

Barbara M. Mitra

This book has provided historical analysis, using the online digital archive of Kays Catalogue, by exploring themes of gendered discourses that emerge through the advertising in the Catalogue. With the rise of new media and online shopping, one could easily assume that there has been a change in relation to how gender is portrayed in advertising. However, academic research suggests that there has been a tendency for offline gender stereotypes to be replicated in the online world, where gender is 'reinscribed in an even more narrow, conventional way' (Milestone and Meyer, 2012: 194). At the same time, the internet also provides a way for people to communicate and collaborate that can challenge the mainstream stereotypes and act as a basis for some alternative discourses (Alrayes and Sutcliffe, 2011: 4). These alternative forums act as impetus for advertisers to think about and perhaps challenge the gender stereotypes in their marketing of certain products.

Catalogue shopping has been overtaken, and superseded in many cases, by the online world which provides more marketing and advertising opportunities. The internet has expanded the range and type of shopping that is available to many people. Advertising is still about 'grabbing the attention of as many people as possible with a view to selling them something' (Mayne, 2000: 56), whether online or offline. In both cases, there are still discourses that are sold alongside clothing and toys and these may influence people in terms of their perceived gender appropriate behaviour. In this chapter, I explore whether gender stereotypes dominate cyberspace or whether cyberspace is proving to be an arena for challenging such stereotypes.

Gender Stereotypes Online

In order to understand whether there is a continuity between stereotypes offline and online, I have examined the Littlewoods website, the Catalogue that amalgamated with Kays in 2003 (see World of Kays Website). The words that surround various advertisements still reveal gendered discourses which continue those found in the digital archive of Kays Catalogue. For example, the notion of a particular body image is still prevalent for women in the online world. Customers are supplied with the female image of a thin body shape through the wording and images in the online Catalogue. If women are unable to conform to the image, they are offered clothing to cover up the shame of not being thin. In advertising holiday clothing for women, the words note that 'In our Holiday Shop you'll find flattering and supportive bikinis, tankinis, kaftans and tunics... and our celebrity range lets you recreate the same looks as gorgeous stars like Fearne Cotton, Kimberley Walsh and Myleene Klass' (Littlewoods Online, 2014). This also reinforces the notion that women should be concerned with how they look and that looking 'gorgeous' is something they need to aim for. Similarly, words such 'When it's time to dress to impress' again suggests that women are encouraged to evaluate themselves by how others see them, including an absent male that is alluded to. Thus, the notion of a thin body shape continues in the online world and may impact negatively on women (e.g. see Wykes and Gunter, 2005 in relation to anorexia and media messages). Plus sizes start from size 14 and although the Catalogue may tell women to 'love their curves', the images used to advertise these clothes still reinforce a thin body ideal. The clothing for working women assumes that women will be in '9 to 5' jobs and highlight being looked at: 'Give your 9 to 5 style a fresh new update. From dresses to jackets, you'll turn heads at the photocopier' (Littlewoods Online, 2014). This assumes that work is of secondary importance to how a woman looks, as well as implying that women will be doing inferior work. Similar assumptions are made in relation to exercise: 'whether you're hitting the gym, running or love yoga, we've all the exercise kit you need' and 'want to look stylish while burning those extra calories...ideal for the keen sportswoman and your casual keep fitter who loves to jump around at her local aerobics dance class' (Littlewoods Online, 2014). This suggests the kind of sporting activities that are suitable for women include: yoga, keep fit, aerobics and dance. Whatever activity women undertake, the advertising suggests, it is important for them to look good whilst doing it and use the activity in order to become attractive. There is far less about women being professional or serious competitors in relation to sports.

Men's fashions in the Catalogue highlight brands and being stylish. The words still suggest that men will be working; an aspect represented by the men's clothing range. They note: 'Our fantastic collection of men's clothes features a variety of practical and stylish wardrobe essentials.... whether you're looking for something smart for the office, or a casual look for a night out, there's something for every occasion in our men's range' (Littlewoods Online, 2014). This speaks to the different versions of masculinity that were highlighted in the Kays Catalogues (such as the working man). Some of the categories included in the Catalogue incorporate a 'Football Fever' section, 'Boats, shoes and espadrilles and Jack Jones brand.' There is the implication that men will do these activities for fun and leisure, whereas women take up fitness (rather than sports) activities in order to look a certain way.

There is a whole section for 'suits', whilst there is no category of 'suits' for women. The men's suits fall into three different styles, offering slightly differing versions of masculinities. The wording for suits notes: 'whether you're looking for a sleek slim fit suit or a classic regular fit, the following suit guide will help you decide which is the best cut and silhouette for you. Let's get smart' (Littlewoods Online 2014). This suggests that men can choose from the particular versions of masculinities on offer. For example, one suit notes: 'A classic tailored suit is the perfect option which you need to look sharp for work or a special occasion' (Littlewoods Online 2014). The word modern also features, with the modern man being another version of masculinity on offer. The slim fit suit 'Has a modern feel with a shorter jacket length, narrower chest, shoulder and waist' (Littlewoods Online 2014). This accentuates that there are different masculinities, (Connell, 2002) rather than one version of masculinity, on offer in the advertising. Leisure is still very much present in relation to the clothing for men in the online Littlewoods Catalogue. For example, the advertisement for football clothing notes that 'If you love to play the beautiful game then make sure you've got all the right kit so you can perform at your very best' (Littlewoods Online 2014). As well as football, there is more general leisure wear: 'whether you're hitting the gym or taking to the pitch we've everything you need to put in a great performance' (Littlewoods Online 2014). For men, sport is about staying in shape, performance and competitiveness compared with the focus on looks for women. Thus the leisure range for men seems to take sports and fitness more seriously than 'jumping around' suggests for children or looking good implies for women.

When looking at the wording surrounding clothing advertising aimed at girls and boys, it is again apparent that the traditional gender stereotypes found in Kays Catalogue were still present in 2014 in the online Littlewoods Catalogue. For example, the wording that advertised clothing for girls noted: 'We've lots of gorgeous new looks for pretty little fashionistas. [...] Trendy clothes are just as important to girls as they are to women, so make sure your daughters' wardrobe is kitted out in the latest styles, trends and fashions' (Littlewoods Online 2014). This continues the gender stereotypes that girls need to be fashionable, aware of how they look, be trendy and adorable. The way that girls are addressed is still about girls who will become women rather than girls being a category in their own right. Most of the dressing up clothes for girls features princesses (such as Rose Princess) and Disney characters (such as Cinderella and Sleeping Beauty). There is also a relational differentiation between boys and girls which continues

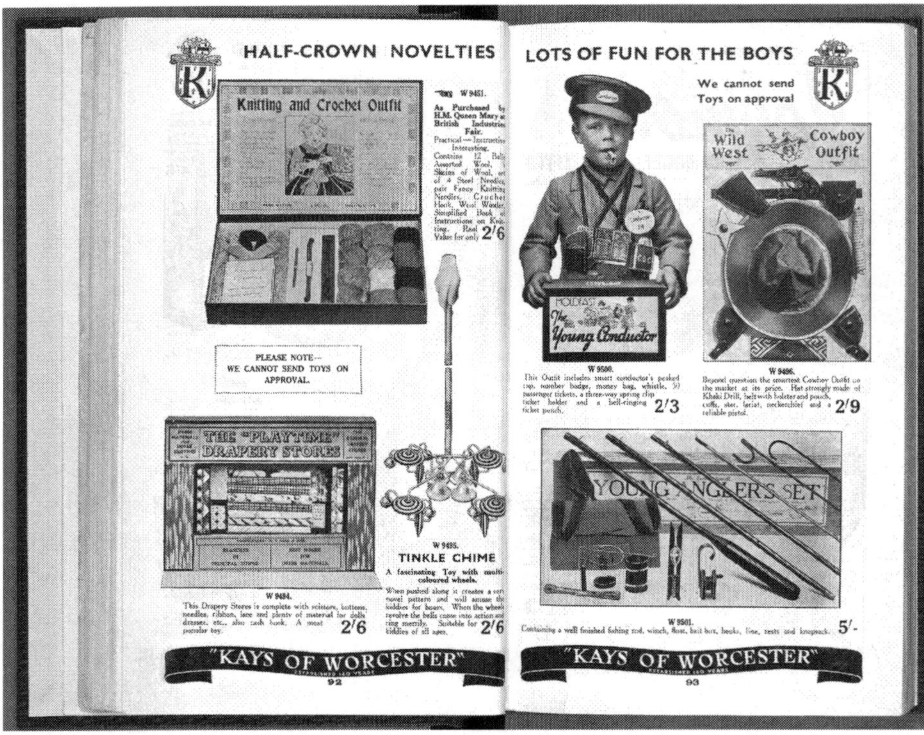

(Kays Catalogue, 1937:92, Autumn and Winter)

with Sportswear in the online Littlewoods Catalogue, where girls are able to choose from Pineapple Girls Dance Crop Pants and Pineapple T Shirts compared with boys who can choose from such items as football and rugby England shirts. (For those unfamiliar with the range, Pineapple is a dance studio in London).

Similarly, advertising for boys continues to promote stereotypes of masculinity: 'Our huge range of boys clothes features everything your sons will need to keep them comfortable, warm and on trend... from smart shirts for family parties to shorts for beach holidays' (Littlewoods Online, 2014). This advertisement emphasises that boys will be doing things, as opposed to the advertisements for girls which suggests that girls need to be concerned with how they look. Boys Fancy Dress included different characters, such as Boys Muscle Chest Superman Costume, Crusader Knight, Deluxe Wolverine and The Invincible Iron Man Muscle Chest. The range highlights stereotypes of muscles and masculinity as something for boys to aspire to. The theme of boys needing hard wearing clothing reiterates the assumption that they will be playing rough games: 'Jeans are just one of those items that are essential in every boy's wardrobe. Our fantastic collections are extremely hard wearing so no matter how roughly he plays they're sure to last a long time' (Littlewoods Online, 2014). This perpetuates the myth that boys should be playing, and playing rough, making a subtle hint about aggression and gender. This is very different from how jeans for girls are advertised: 'Trendy girls' jeans in colours your daughter will love, styles she'll adore and designs she'll be truly passionate about' (Littlewoods Online, 2014). Thus, boys and girls are taught through the clothing advertising that they should perceive of themselves as being different to each other, doing different things and behaving differently. The Catalogue also communicates that the category of boy/girl is relational where boys are treated as a category in their own right whilst girls are treated as future women.

As the examples analysed above indicate, just as gender involves 'continuously and consistently acting and expressing yourself in a way that fits the conventional script of gender' (Donath, 1999 cited in Milestone and Meyer, 2012), advertising companies themselves consistently and continuously address males and females in ways that fit the conventional scripts of gender. This has been the case in the printed Kays Catalogue and is still the case, in most instances, in the online world of Internet shopping. One only has to look at the Littlewoods website to find purple ironing boards and pink Hetty vacuum cleaners. As Herring and Paolillo (2006) note, language used online reflects very traditional stereotypes of gender and for the most part advertising online replicates those stereotypes.

The advertisements for toys continue some stereotypes whilst others are slightly challenged. For example, the doll advertisements highlight that these are exclusively for girls: 'Make sure you get all the best accessories for your daughter's new doll. We have a huge range of dolls' prams and accessories so that your little girl will be able to provide the perfect outfit, home and transport for her dolls' (Littlewoods Online, 2014). However, under the advertisements for 'Cars, Planes and Trains', it is assumed that girls may also be interested in these type of toys with words such as: 'If your little boy or girl is obsessed with cars then we've got the toy cars that will make perfect additions to their collection. We have a variety of fun designs ranging from TV character themes to exciting sporting cars, remote controlled racers to whole scalextric kits. Get your kids on the road from an early age with our superb toy cars' (Littlewoods Online, 2014), indicating that advertising discourses have changed. This may also reflect that film and television companies such as Warner Bros. have developed their own divisions to market toys and often hope to attract both genders to ensure greater financial rewards (Miller, 1995). In some respects, the advertisements suggest that while it is still not acceptable for boys to like toys for girls, it is acceptable for girls to like toys for boys (see Mitra and Lewin-Jones, 2012).

Stereotypes challenged

The internet, though, has also provided a forum for such gender distinctions and stereotypes to be challenged and for the online world to provide a place for discussion and alternative discourses. In recent years, gender-specific marketing has gained media attention – such as the 'Bic for her' pen, or a science kit for children being put in the 'toys for boys' section (in Sainsbury's) and its 'boys' label causing much controversy and criticism during 2013. The internet provides the arena for debates and complaints which by gathering momentum can challenge such gendered marketing. For example, the Pinkstinks campaign has gained much media attention. Founded in London in May 2008, this campaign aims to raise awareness of what it claims is damage caused by gender stereotyping of children, particularly in encouraging girls to limit their ambitions later in life. The website contains a list of approved companies that provide non-gender specific play and learning products for children. The campaign has inspired other similar movements and protests such as the outcry against a doctor's outfit being labelled for boys, and nurse and beautician outfits being labelled for girls in Sainsbury's supermarkets in 2014. Similarly, there was a campaign against the marketing of make-up by Fisher-Price in 2012 to the under 3 age group and padded bras (2011) being marketed to very young girls (Matalan advertised these as being from age 3-13 years). Thus the online world, then, can provide alternative discourses in relation to gender although mainstream gender norms generally tend to dominate.

Most shops that sell toys tend to have aisles clearly demarcated for boys and girls. In Stockholm, the store 'Toys R Us' warehouses no longer have such demarcated isles. Instead of conforming to the code pink and purple for girls, and blue and dark colours for boys, children, it is argued, should be 'free to choose what they want to play with' (Crouch, 2013). 'Toys R Us' have published gender neutral catalogues in Finland, Norway, Germany, Denmark and France (Crouch, 2013). They have also stopped labelling toys as being for boys and girls. It seems that the marketing of toys is becoming an area where gender stereotypes are beginning to be challenged. Nevertheless, clothing still seems to be steeped in stereotypes in relation to gender and advertising. The role of the internet in gathering support for various causes has been noted (see Webster, 2014) and perhaps this has helped some of the campaigns. Despite these examples, mainstream gender norms continue to dominate both the offline and online worlds.

The internet also enables women to find other organisations that challenge gender stereotypes, such as Women in Film & Television International which

(Kays Catalogue, 1950: 128, Spring and Summer)

is a global network encouraging advancing professional development and achievement of women. Women in Advertising and Communications is a group of women in the UK Communications Industry organised to network, inspire and support each other. Another magazine that is purely online and crowd funded is *Feminist Times*. Their website notes that 'Fem T is a precious space where brands don't influence content...', they advocate to 'Be part of 3D feminism' (Feminist Times Online, 2014), and highlight how discourses tend to reinforce gender stereotypes particularly for women. The online magazine aimed at interesting women and raising feminist issues, is a 'place where people can detox from mainstream media culture... I have broken my Grazia and Mail Online habit.... Our desire to plug into the collective female consciousness is ideological not simply pragmatic' (Feminist Times Online, 2014). These websites and alternative discourses about gender may attract those who would challenge such stereotypes in any case. That said, some campaigns have gathered enough momentum to confront the marketing practices of companies and to cause them to make some changes in how they address males and females. These may be small changes, such as three female scientist figures being produced by Lego, but they are nevertheless changes. As advertising continues to permeate both the online and offline worlds, let us hope that future marketing will not be steeped in stereotypes but will promote a wider range of discourses relating to gender.

Conclusion

Online Catalogue advertisements aimed at adults still tend to reinforce gender stereotypes as the analysis of the Littlewoods Catalogue shows, where there are clear differences between the ways in which men and women are addressed. The world of toys is changing, albeit slowly, where there are efforts to raise awareness that making toys gender specific may encourage boys and girls to perceive themselves (and what they are able to achieve) in particular ways. While the online world tends to emphasise stereotypes, there are pockets of alternative discourses in relation to gender which enables us to be slightly optimistic for the future.

References

Alrayes, A. and Sutcliffe, A. (2011) Students' Attitudes in a Virtual Environment. *Virtual Worlds Research.* Vol. 4(1), pp. 3-17.
Connell, R. W. (2002) *Gender.* Cambridge, Polity.
Crouch, D. (2013) Toys R Us's Stockholm superstore goes gender neutral. *The Guardian Online* (Monday 23rd December) available at: http://www.theguardian.com/world/2013/dec/23/toys-r-us-stockholm-gender-neutral] Accessed 30/4/2014.
Donath, J. S. (1999) Identity and deception in the virtual community in M.A. Smith and P. Kollock (eds.) *Communities in Cyberspace*, London: Routledge.
Herring, S.C. and Paolillo, J.C. (2006) Gender and genre variation in weblogs. *Journal of Sociolinguistics.* Vol. 10(4), pp.439-459.
Mayne, I. (2000) The Inescapable Images. Gender and Advertising. *Equal Opportunities International.* Vol. 19(2/3/4), pp.56-61.
Milestone, K. and Meyer, A. (2012) *Gender & Popular Culture.* Cambridge: Polity.
Miller, C. (1995) Tinseltown Toys are Tops. *Marketing News.* Vol. 29(25), pp.1, 15.
Mitra, B. and Lewin-Jones, J. (2012) Colin won't drink out of a pink cup, in K. Ross (ed.) *Blackwell Handbook of Gender Sexualities and the Media.* Oxford. Wiley-Blackwell, pp.383-400.
Webster, F. (2014) *Theories of the Information Society.* Fourth edition. Oxon, Routledge.
Wykes, M. and Gunter, B. (2005) *The Media & Body Image.* London, Sage.

Websites

Feminist Times http://www.feministtimes.com/
Littlewoods Online http://www.littlewoods.com/
Pinkstinks http://www.pinkstinks.co.uk/
Women in Advertising and Communication http://www.wacl.info/
Women in Film and Television http://www.wift.org/about/index.html
World of Kays http://www.worldofkays.org/

// Index //